Depression Era Dime Store

Kitchen, Home, and Garden

Revised 2nd Edition

C.L. Miller

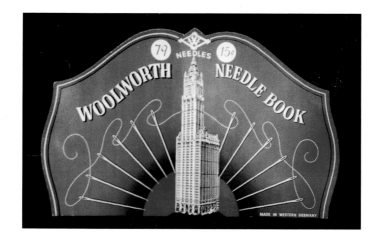

4880 Lower Valley Road, Atglen, PA 19310 USA

Title page photo: The Woolworth Needle Book had seventy-nine assorted needles and sold for 15¢. *Davis Collection.* $15-$20.

Revised price guide: 2001
Copyright © 2000 & 2001 by C.L. Miller
Library of Congress Catalog Card Number: 2001086055

Designed by "Sue"
Type set in Bodoni Bd BT/Aldine 721 BT

ISBN: 0-7643-1374-6
Printed in China
1 2 3 4

Published by Schiffer Publishing Ltd.
4880 Lower Valley Road
Atglen, PA 19310
Phone: (610) 593-1777; Fax: (610) 593-2002
E-mail: Schifferbk@aol.com
Please visit our web site catalog at
www.schifferbooks.com

This book may be purchased from the publisher.
Include $3.95 for shipping. Please try your bookstore first.
We are always looking for people to write books on new and related subjects. If you have an idea for a book please contact us at the above address.
You may write for a free catalog.

In Europe, Schiffer books are distributed by
Bushwood Books
6 Marksbury Avenue
Kew Gardens
Surrey TW9 4JF England
Phone: 44 (0) 20-8392-8585; Fax: 44 (0) 20-8392-9876
E-mail: Bushwd@aol.com
Free postage in the UK. Europe: air mail at cost.

Contents

3 DESIGNS—3 COLORS

Dedication

To Lula Miller Heffelfinger and a Halloween rabbit costume she purchased for me in 1946 from the Schultz's Bros., Five-and-Ten-Cent-Store in Hoopeston, Illinois.

Acknowledgments

My appreciation to each of the following for their support and contributions during the development of this publication. Rod and Sally Blackstone, Dan and Debbie Breeding, Cambria County Library System of Johnstown, Pennsylvania, Stephen J. and Mary Caye Clark, Julie Collart, Russ and Donna Colwell, Columbus Public Library of Columbus, Ohio, James L. Cooper, Ann C. Davis, Douglas B. Dupler, Ela Area Public Library of Lake Zurich, Illinois, Ela Historical Society, Lake Zurich, Illinois, Mrs. Walter Evans, Karen L. Evans, Sadie B. Evans, Larry Flinchpaugh, Carolyn K. Frash, Lisa M. Gonzalez, Mary Ann Heft, Gloria B. Heramb, Hoopeston Public Library of Hoopeston, Illinois, Larry and Karen Kanter, Merry Palicz, Lynn Public Library of Lynn, Massachusetts. Casey and Chris McGowan, Joan E. Neel, Kay Neer, David M. and Jill M. Nelson, Carl and Bonnie Riddlebarger, Byron Rider, Rochester Public Library (Local History Division) Rochester, New York, Mike and Cindy Schneider, Suzanne Studer, Todd Turner, The Cherubs Chest Awesome Antiques-Royal Oak, Michigan, Nancy J. Weller, Steve P. and Jackie J. Wolfe, Stephanie J. Wolfe, Stan and Karen Zera. If I have overlooked anyone, I apologize at this time.

Foreword

This book is designed to aid collectors in recognizing merchandise for the kitchen, home, and garden that was available or associated with any five-and-ten-cent store, whether it was Ben Franklin, H.L. Green, W.T. Grant's, S.S. Kresge, S.H. Kress, McCrory, McLellan, G.C. Murphy, J.J. Newberry, Neisner's, Lamston, Schultz's Bros., or F.W. Woolworth's. These stores were once a staple item along "Main Street, U.S.A." and the china, cookware, and other household merchandise they carried has become highly collectible. In preparing this book, I have provided information available from my own records and those made possible through other sources. If I have made mistakes or mislead anyone, I apologize at this time.

Some time ago, I retrieved an original 1939-1943 wholesale distribution catalogue from an old storage trunk at a local flea market. It listed various merchandise that was available to many of the five-and ten-cent stores, and many of those original documents and/or photographs appear throughout this publication. The original text from this catalogue provided captions, dates, and retail prices. Without those records this project could never have been undertaken.

Whether you are a novice or already a serious collector of dime store memorabilia, I hope you enjoy this publication and I invite you to examine and enjoy the counters of the five-and-ten-cent stores.

Introduction

I grew up during the 1940s and 1950s peering through the front windows of two American icons: the local G.C. Murphy Co., and Schultz's Bros., Five-and-Ten-Cent Stores in Hoopeston, Illinois. Both are now closed and the marquees that once spelled out their famous trademarks have been removed. A new generation occupies one store; the only remains of the once thriving G.C. Murphy Co., is a vacant lot.

On a Saturday morning in 1946, after getting all dressed up, I accompanied my mother and my aunt on a shopping trip into the business district of this Illinois community. We started at one end of the business section and would eventually finish at the opposite end. At the utility company, an envelope containing a bill with a check and/or cash was pushed through the slot provided by the company, then on we walked in the direction of the next business transaction where another envelope fell into another slot. All business transactions and banking at "City National" had to be taken care of first before any other shopping was completed.

In most small towns everyone knew everyone else and it was no different in this Illinois community. These weekly trips were always interrupted by an unexpected encounter with a neighbor, friend, or family member downtown. For many it was a social gathering, for others it was an erudite account of events . . . it was Main Street USA, a way of life.

The author and his mother, taken January 1946, in front of the G.C. Murphy Company Five-and-Ten-Cent-Store in Hoopeston, Illinois.

Main Street, U.S.A.

Car horns echoed up and down Main Street and off in the distance a shrill whistle signaled the approach of a train. Stores along Main Street boomed with business as men and women hurried from one store to another along the few blocks of the popular business district. Children on bicycles moved in and out of traffic, headed to one of the local theaters or to the public library. Dogs lapped at the overflow of water at the base of the corner granite water fountain and teenagers gathered at the local "Sugar Bowl" restaurant.

At the Lorraine Theatre the marquee advertised Bette Davis in "Her Greatest Performance!" starring in *The Corn is Green* with John Dall and Joan Lorring. Down at the Princess Theatre, Bob Steele and a host of other stars were appearing in *The Navajo Kid*. The price of admission at either theater was 12¢ for children and 25¢ for adults. I was too young to understand the artistry of Bette Davis, and the Princess Theater was showing only two shows each night, one at 7:15 and the other at 9:00, which was too late. Mother was somewhat uncertain of a child seeing *Navajo Kid*, so I would have to settle for a sundae at the local "Ritz" restaurant and then we would check out the merchandise at the "no-

MAIN STREET LOOKING WEST, HOOPESTON, ILLINOIS   F-573

Postcard of Main Street in Hoopeston, Illinois, where Schultz's Bros., and G.C. Murphy's were both located. $10-$18.

tions" counter at both five-and-ten-cent stores. In our town we were not fortunate enough to have a dime store that had a luncheonette counter; those stores—H.L. Green, W.T. Grant's, S.S. Kresge's, S.H. Kress, McCrory, F.W. Woolworth, and other trademark names—were located in major cities.

Most residents depended on one of the two five-and-ten-cent stores for many necessities. Assorted china, glassware, pots and pans, candy, bobby pins, Tangee, Bourjois Evening In Paris, June Knight, Blue Waltz or April Showers, cosmetic preparations, hairnets, goldfish and pet supplies, bib overalls, baby clothes, Fitch's products for men, greeting cards, postcards, and toys were all displayed temptingly. For teen-agers, the latest in fad merchandise, records, glamour magazines, cosmetics, and costume jewelry was available.

Schultz's Bros.

It was in 1946 at Schultz's Bros., Five-and-Ten-Cent-Store that my first Halloween costume was purchased by my aunt, to whom I have dedicated this book. It was a cheaply made, one-piece pink costume of cambric material that had an attached stubby tail and a opening in the back with a drawstring to secure it around the neck. The costume came individually boxed in a colorful window carton adorned with dancing rabbits. Enclosed was the cloth mask with two large black openings for the eyes, rosy cheeks splashed in red on either side of the face, and a small white nose surrounded by long synthetic whiskers.

This humorous rabbit mask with its long pink ears was made of a gauze-like material and was held in place by a lone rubber band that would break before I got one season's wear out of it. The stiff mask clung to my face and as I exhaled moisture gathered against the surface; within an hour the structure of the rabbit's face had collapsed and the once smiling rabbit had turned into a saturated soggy mess.

The primary entrance for Schultz's Bros., Five-and-Ten-Cent Store was located in the center of a narrow building located on the south side of Main Street; directly across the street on the north side was the G.C. Murphy Co. It was not uncommon for dime stores to be established across the street or next to each other.

Entering Schultz's Bros., shoppers first noticed the large U-shaped, three section slanted glass candy counter that held an assortment of bulk candy, fancy prepackaged chocolates, and hot roasted peanuts, rotating on a divided round tray. Behind the counter a young high school clerk referred to as a "Salesgirl" weighed out each pound on the scales located nearby. It is believed the term "Salesgirl" was coined by F.W. Woolworth. There was always a salesgirl ready to wait on everyone.

G.C. Murphy Co.

The G.C. Murphy Co. was the larger of the two stores and offered three entrances to the building. The store's large front windows were displayed with the latest merchandise available to clientele. A larger, U-shaped slanted glass front candy counter was located in the main section, surrounded by the latest notions, fashionable jewelry, cosmetics, and garments for both women, men, babies, and young adults.

On August 18, 1947, B.F. Short became the new manager of the G.C. Murphy Stores in Hoopeston, Illinois. Mr. Short had been with the five-and-dime chain for thirteen years and came to the Hoopeston store from Shelbyville, Indiana to replace O.J. Gregg. Short served as assistant manager of several Ohio and Indiana stores.

Postcard showing the G. C. Murphy store and restaurant in downtown Streator, Illinois, not far from the author's hometown of Hoopeston.

A Shopper's Paradise

When sales advertisements for either of the stores appeared in the local paper, the crowd that gathered was a crowd in a hurry to get to either of the stores first. They thrust money at the clerk, they shouted at salesgirls as they tried to acquire one of the big advertised bargains. To these shoppers, it was Mecca.

A salesgirl handling these crowds had to be resourceful, deliberate, and cool headed. Usually it was necessary to have someone assist the salesgirl in making change, wrapping and handling merchandise. Most bargain items were too few and the store ran out too quickly. The manager knew it was far better to have too few than too many, to avoid ending up with an excess.

Display Windows

Peering through the front windows of either of these stores provided only a hint of the contents displayed inside, which changed with the seasons or the approaching holidays.

"L" shaped windows were the most popular and desirable to have since these windows increased store sales. Most major stores had "L" shaped windows and they were trimmed with merchandise. Window trims were changed frequently and anything left for over two weeks was a neglect in sales possibilities.

Panes of glass were first used in store fronts, in order to allow light in and to classify a store. As the number of stores next to each other increased, it became convenient for them to identify their own store by hanging certain items sold in their front windows. Over time, the pane windows became a "solid" plate glass front designed for the display of merchandise. A "solid" window was used to display a larger volume of merchandise.

Window displays were designed to impress the traffic that passed by and to draw them into the store. To stimulate and increase business, the common "solid" window items were: enamelware, aluminum ware, towels, silk hose, stamped dresser scarfs, men's work shirts, straw hats, house shoes, chair seats, wash boards, galvanized pails, brooms, underwear, and millinery flowers.

There were three types of displays for store windows. Windows containing goods sold as loss leaders were called "feature" windows; windows containing regular goods of one class or type that sold regularly at a profit were called "solid" windows; windows of assorted or general merchandise from the regular run of the stock were called "mixed" or "regular" windows.

In 1924, S.S. Kresge provided a small, thirty-six page guidebook to their employees. The *Kresge Job Ahead* was an aid to men in training; should an employee leave, the guidebook was to be returned to the store manager. This guidebook emphasized the importance of window trimming and the source of great profit if properly done. Window displays were the best form of advertising both day and night for the store. Many photographs of S.S. Kresge window displays were taken and sent to all of the stores from their Detroit headquarters. These photographs were to be studied and then implemented.

Seasonal and Holiday Merchandise

Holiday buying each year increased the stores' investment. In many five-and-ten-cent-stores, December sales amounted to 25% of the annual business. Merchandise was displayed long before the holiday arrived, since shoppers as a rule entered a store with more or less frequency. If a shopper noticed seasonable merchandise displayed a number of times before she was ready to buy it, she generally thought of the store in which she had seen it when she was ready to purchase her holiday gifts.

Holiday decorations are in demand among collectors and escalating in price. These colorful decorations have found their way out of the attic and storage boxes into private collections and are now readily available at most antique shows, flea markets, and shops. Especially popular are those for Christmas and Halloween. It is impossible here to provide a complete listing of holiday merchandise available from the five-and-ten-cent stores, however many publications have been written specifically on various holiday decorations—check with your local book dealer.

During August, the windows announced the approaching school year with a display of stationery and art supplies, including major stationery, composition books, loose-leaf tablets, pencil boxes alongside the ever famous Number Two pencils, Carter's ink products in Midnight Black, Sunset Violet, Sunset Green or Sunset Red. Scotch tape was displayed with an assortment of Carter's and Testor's paste, mucilage, and cement; in the opposite window was a selection of the latest school clothes. Today, ink products are readily available at most antique shows, shops and flea markets and are moderately priced.

After the local schools opened, the displays changed to an array of Halloween costumes followed by Thanksgiving decorations, followed by Christmas—the most popular holiday of the year. The Christmas season drew customers to the counters of the five-and-ten to see the magical displays that appeared throughout the store or in the front windows. Tipco Deluxe tinsel seals, striped wrapping paper, bright lights, pine cones, and poinsettia decorations all announced the approaching holiday. As each year passed the windows of the local stores continued to change, displaying new items, necessities and those still favorites among their clientele.

"Merry Christmas to you from Neisner's." This Christmas window display offered an enticing assortment of holiday books, toys, and games. The store's location is unknown. Photograph $30-40.

Salesgirls

Salesgirls made suggestions, could accurately make change, bagged and wrote out a receipt for purchases with care—all for the convenience of every customer. They worked moderately short hours and in a clean, wholesome environment; they were given every opportunity for advancement throughout the company as designers of stores, window displays, department heads, or other responsible office positions. Carefully chosen for their appearance, personality, and character, salesgirls were trained by management in serving the public and took pride in the courteous attention they provided every customer. Often young high school girls, single women, and/or married women of the community sought employment at the local five-and-ten-cent store. They learned fast and took on the responsibility of displaying the merchandise that they also neatly arranged and clearly priced.

One form of pricing used was a metal holder that gave the price of the item and was held in place on the edge of the shelves. Another type of holder used signs that hung on a "T" stand. There were also standard ticket holders designed to stand erect on the back edge of a counter display. There was also a stencil outfit used to make any kind of price tag or sign needed. This outfit was indispensable to merchants who wanted neat prices and cards at various times of the year. Management knew that price tags were the silent "salesmen"—the more price tags, the less questions that required answering. Management required that every item carry a price tag and every display be clearly marked. Window merchandise had to be marked clearly so that any customer "window shopping" had a clear view of the indicated price.

Each salesgirl was responsible for her own cash register in her own section of the store. Salesgirls usually worked under a senior clerk or directly under the store manager. Most stores had a list of "Store Rules and Regulations," which was provided to each employee or posted within easy access. A listing of such store rules and regulations can be found on pages 15-17 of *Depression Era Dime Store Glass* (Schiffer Publishing Ltd., 1999)

In 1925, salesgirls were paid by commission on the basis of weekly sales. It was believed that a salesgirl should sell $135.00 worth of merchandise a week, which was used to establish a base wage of 6-1/2% and equaled $8.78. A bonus of 2-1/2% was often paid on sales over $135.00. For example, if a good salesgirl sold $180.00 worth of merchandise in a week, her compensation would be 6-1/2% of the $180.00 plus 2-1/2% of the $45.00 above her quota, for a total weekly pay of $12.83. Bonus money was only paid to those who observed the rules provided by the store and who kept their sections in excellent conditions.

Salesgirls were responsible for waiting on customers in certain sections assigned to them and were to work only in those sections, unless it was necessary to assist another salesgirl. When customers were not around, many stores required their salesgirls to clean counters and check stock. Many five-and-ten-cent stores insisted upon these procedures.

On busy days it was wise to have salesgirls at stationary locations and behind counters from which they could depart; other salesgirls were placed at stationary locations where shrinkage was most likely to occur . . . the jewelry counter, toy counter, and the notions counter.

This original photograph of salesclerks and managers is dated January 6, 1942 and is believed to have been taken in the Home and Garden department of F.W. Woolworth store number 674. Store number 674 was located at 3735 Lexington Road, Louisville, Kentucky. *Author's Collection.* $30-40.

Shrinkage

Every employee within the store was expected to acquire a reputation for being watchful and for constantly observing their customers and their actions. Salesgirls were warned to pay close attention for shoplifting, one of the problems that resulted in shrinkage.

For many stores, little boys were often held in suspicion of shoplifting. There were no age limits or color lines to be drawn when it came to shoplifting. Many stores soon developed a reputation as being a "tough" store from which to steal.

Certain types of merchandise were popular among people who shoplifted. Small articles of jewelry, for example, were easy to pick up and conceal. Pencils, pocket knives, harmonicas, perfume, compacts, lipsticks, hose, handkerchiefs, and other items were to be watched constantly. Ladies' hose were rolled and then slipped into a pocket, handbag, or up a sleeve.

Shoplifters usually took advantage of times when the store was crowded with people and the salesgirls were the busiest. Management urged all salesgirls to be careful in dealing with shoplifters and to be sure of themselves, making no accusations that could open liability charges for damages in the event the store would lose the case.

Another form of shrinkage resulting in a considerable amount of loss came directly from within the store: appropriation of merchandise by salesgirls for personal use. This was a common practice in older stores. Store personnel took it for granted that they could have any reasonable amount of merchandise for personal use or consumption. Within one year, a salesgirl could consume a considerable portion of what should have been net profit, most commonly through eating candy and also through the appropriation of powder, compacts, powder puffs, nail files, scissors, safety pins, soap, sanitary goods, and cosmetics in general. Such appropriation was a direct, irremediable loss.

Breakage was another form of shrinkage and was unavoidable in any dime store. It resulted from the unpacking and marking of goods, handling of merchandise on the counters, and damage to goods through depreciation causing counter wear. The ends of thread came loose and began to appear soiled. Goods placed in windows began to fade. Elastic supporters deteriorated quickly and ribbon became tender as it aged and dried out in direct sunlight. Jewelry, tarnished and broken, was often sold at bargain prices. Some merchandise became "shopworn" and the store accepted a lesser price. Managers were often instructed to buy only in modest quantities in order for merchandise to last a reasonable time.

Store Plans

All salesgirls were required to become familiar with the layout of the store and the arrangement of the merchandise.

Schultz's Bros. had two major aisles that ran the length of the store, with crossover sections linking the two aisles together. The counters were of the same width throughout. Merchandise sold from the dime stores was actually sold from counters throughout the store, and from them only. Counters conveniently displayed what customers were looking for, with price tickets answering their unasked questions. Omitting prices resulted in lost sales.

Merchandise that had been out for a few days became soiled and depreciated, looked unclean, and sold slower. Salesgirls followed the rule of the store and sold the oldest merchandise first.

Damaged goods were never put with good merchandise. A separate display accompanied by a sign explaining their presence and a notation that the merchandise was available at a price reduction often saved the reputation of the store. Customers could become suspicious if damaged merchandise was mixed with good.

Counter paper was often used by the best dime stores to line trays in which the merchandise was displayed. The use of this paper made merchandise look more inviting and set merchandise off to an advantage. Counter paper was available to fit trays and counter widths in all standard sizes. The majority of dime stores acquired this paper from "Butler Brothers," a wholesale distributor referred to as the "Jobber."

BUTLER BROTHERS BUILDING, DALLAS, TEXAS.   19902

This postcard, dated March 10, 1942, shows the Butler Brothers Building in Dallas, Texas. Author's Collection. $15-20.

Items that were related to one another were displayed side by side, in order that the sale of one could help the sale of the other. Toothpaste and toothbrushes, hosiery and garters, window shades and curtain rods, and similar household articles were kept together. Face powders, compacts, and powder puffs were displayed together as were nail brushes and soap. Hair brushes, however, were never displayed with scrub brushes. Managers were often advised to avoid grotesque and incongruous combinations, which killed trade.

Near the back of Schultz's Bros., just past the creak in the floor, was a small pet section with tanks of swimming goldfish, a cage of yellow singing canaries, an assortment of bird and fish food, gravel paper, cedar perches, skin ointments, and an array of various pet supplies and pet toys. Today, only pet products of ornate design, unusual decoration, and/ or rarity are escalating in price and demand.

Most children could be found in the pet section of any dime store—or across the aisle looking at celluloid toys, beautifully illustrated puzzles, and "Golden" books. It was also in this section where sheet music and household accessories were located. Celluloid toys, puzzles, and novelties items are highly collectible. Many puzzle collectors search for those of various categories: in a series, specific artist or illustrator, maps, and numbered.

It was habit that brought customers back and forth across the street to either one of the local dime stores. What couldn't be found in one was sure to be found in the other. Up and down the aisles the world of the five-and-ten-cent store revolved.

Inside view of a Kresge store. Cannon wash cloths and dish cloths, Talon slide fasteners, and Clark's sewing threads are among the goods on display. *Private Collection.*

Postcard showing interior of The Kress 5, 10 and 25¢ Store in Hot Springs, Arkansas. $10-$15.

The Jewelry and Candy Counters

Jewelry was one of the most profitable items that a dime store could handle.

There were two desirable types of jewelry counters. One was a "U" shaped counter, which was found in most major stores. The other was a straight case similar to an end counter. A glass-covered jewelry display case secured a better effect and made the jewelry section more profitable by cutting down on shrinkage.

Several kinds of candy cases were recommended for five-and-ten-cent stores. The old-fashioned cases left candy unprotected, resulting in losses of sales. They were more expensive in the long run to operate than the newer cases, which protected the contents and cut down on waste. No store could afford a candy case that permitted hands, flies, insects, or rodents easy access. Christmas, Valentine's Day, and Easter were the most popular holidays at the candy counter. An early supplier of candy was Auerbach & Sons, of Cincinnati, Ohio.

In 1925, the most popular selling candy in any five-and-ten cent store was plain vanilla, chocolate, and marbled fudge, large jelly drops, peanut butter kisses, molasses kisses, jelly beans, wrapped caramels, plain white

19

marshmallows, toasted marshmallows, chocolate drops, chocolate pralines, circus peanuts (yellow only), salted peanuts, and peanut squares (winter season only).

In cold weather only, dime stores offered a large assortment of high grade chocolates, including chocolate caramels, nougat, and chips. Chocolate creams were available with assorted flavor centers of vanilla, lemon, strawberry, raspberry, maple, and whipped cream. An assortment of chocolate almond bars, chocolate peanut bars, and milk chocolate bars sold for 5¢ each, along with Wrigley's Spearmint, Juicy Fruit, and Doublemint gum.

An original 1946 newspaper advertisement for "Murphy's Annual Assistant Mgr. Candy Specials" listed the following for sale: "Fruit and Nut filled Kisses lb., at 40¢, Chocolate Peanut Butter Chips lb., at 50¢, Almond Butter Sticks lb., at 30¢, Peanut Butter Filled Mary Anns lb., 25¢, Peanut Squares lb., 40¢, Licorice Nougat lb., 30¢, Chocolate Cream Loaf lb., 49¢, Chocolate Peanut Clusters lb., 50¢, Creamy Nut Fudge lb., 50¢, Pure Sugar Lollipops 12 for 25¢ and Triumph Bars 2 for 5¢."

A Service Viewpoint

Almost everything that was sold in dime stores could be purchased somewhere else nearby. A customer's first impression of the store was a major selling point and dime stores realized they faced competition, if not for all of their items, at least for a great many of them. Most major stores developed "tact," which meant greater sales. A customer who showed interest in a five-cent item that she purchased, for example, could be the same customer apt to leave the store with ten dollars worth of merchandise—the result of some tactful suggestions.

In 1929, F.W. Woolworth Co. provided customers with a *Home Shopping Guide*, published as part of the company's fiftieth anniversary celebration. It read in part: "This little book has been prepared by the F.W. Woolworth Co. to be of practical service to you and your home. Hang it up in a convenient spot where it may serve always as a friendly reminder. Consult its pages whenever any need arises in your kitchen, your laundry, your pantry, your bathroom, your dressing table, your sewing, your garage or garden, or in any of the thousand and one little emergencies of everyday housekeeping. You will be amazed at the number of articles you can buy for 5¢ or 10¢. Many things once regarded as luxuries can now be bought by your nickels and dimes from Woolworth counters." ©1929, F.W. Woolworth Co. $35-$40.

Women customers enjoyed trying on the latest fashions. If dressing rooms were provided, this sometimes resulted in impulse buying, which meant cash in hand. G.C. Murphy Co. provided two dressing rooms with colorful floral drapes that concealed a dressing client.

An array of the latest fashionable hats of the period was located nearby, where ladies were often seen trying on the newest arrival. Toys, Columbia window shades, oilcloth in various patterns and colors, were located in the rear of the store near an entrance to the basement and the receiving dock.

The Annex

Clientele had access to additional shopping space through two primary entrances into an annex, located east of the main section of the store. Located at the rear of the annex was a small office where everyday business deals, customer satisfaction, and agreements were taken care of.

The five-and-ten-cent stores tried to be sure that all their customers left satisfied. They made refunds and exchanges whenever it was within reason, rather than send the customer away indignant and upset. All salesgirls were instructed that damaged goods sold "as is," however, would have no exchanges or refunds. When refunds *were* cheerfully made, the chances that the money would be immediately spent for additional merchandise in the store were great. Customers first liked to get the money back and actually have it in hand.

If loose change was given and small children were present, the change was often given to those children to use for additional merchandise. In the annex to G.C. Murphy's, for example, there was a mechanical pony. For 5¢ a child rode off into the sunset, and the cost of that ride may very well have been provided by the refund change. This resulted in another happy customer—a satisfied child—as well as the money being returned to the five-and-ten-cent-store.

So many of the items purchased from the counters at the local five-and-ten-cent stores are lost to time. My only regret is that once I became an adult and moved away, I never went back through those doors or peered into those windows that were once a big part of my childhood—and that my family and this Illinois community had depended upon. By then, like so many others, I had become accustomed to shopping malls, having acquired a taste for designer clothes, expensive toiletries, and accessories. Those items could not be found at the local five-and-ten-cent stores, stores that were the anchor of our American "Main Street" and now represent the end of an era. It is disheartening to think that so many of us gave them up for suburban malls, outlets, discount houses, and free parking.

I no longer have the cheaply made rabbit Halloween costume with the soggy mask. For some reason, days after I carried it home and modeled it for my grandparents, I took it off, carried it behind an out building, and saturated the costume and what was left of the mask with water.

Remember this famous mechanical pony? A ride on the "Pony Express" at Kresge cost only 5¢. Mechanical Pony $2,000-$2,500 complete.

Part I

The Kitchen Aisles

Dinnerware and Tableware

In "Kresge's Katalog of 5¢ and 10¢ Merchandise" ©1913 and 1975, three patterns of open stock dinnerware could be ordered directly from the S.S. Kresge Company for only 5¢ and 10¢ per piece. Although photographs of these three patterns are not available, their decorations and the shapes that were available are described below.

Gold Loop pattern was a pure white, semi-porcelain with fast under glazed colors. The dinnerware was made of the best imported clay from England and made in the largest china companies of America. Each piece is decorated with a continuous gold loop pattern and gold edge. The pattern included a fruit saucer, oatmeal dish, bread and butter plate, pie plate, tea plate, soup plate, dinner plate, 6" salad bowl, 7" salad bowl, 6" oval baker, 7" oval baker, 7" x 10" platter, 8" x 10-3/4" platter, 9" x 11-3/4" platter, creamer, fancy bowl, cup and saucer. Manufacturer and marking are unknown.

Morning Glory pattern was decorated with beautiful morning glory vine and flowers with a gold edge and fast under glazed colors. This dinnerware was also made of the best imported clay from England and made in the largest china companies of America. Available was a fruit saucer, oatmeal dish, bread and butter plate, pie plate, tea plate, soup plate, dinner plate, 2-1/2" x 6" salad bowl, 3" x 7" salad bowl, 6" oval baker, 7" oval baker, 7" platter, 8" platter, 9" x 11-3/4" platter, creamer, fancy bowl, cup and saucer. Manufacturer and marking are unknown.

Flow Blue pattern was an under glazed dinnerware illustrated in the "Katalog of 5¢ and 10¢ Merchandise." Made of high-grade imported clay, the pattern was decorated with a dark blue edge, graduating into a lighter shade of blue with a gold edge and gold decorations over the blue. This set of Flow Blue pattern dinnerware included a 4" fruit dish, 5" fruit dish, tea plate, dinner plate, 7" nappy, soup plate, baker, 7" x 11" platter, bowl, jug, cup and saucer. Manufacturer and marking are unknown.

Kresge's "Truck-Load Sale" featured "White Cups 6¢," circa 1940s-1950s. Note the two styles of white cups in this historical photograph. Kresge supplied one of the largest demands for china through their own suppliers. Photograph $50-$60.

Colonial Garland Pattern

"Colonial Garland" pattern was an exclusive Ben Franklin dinnerware. This pattern will be backstamped "Franklinware-U.S.A." All Colonial Garland pieces were available in any quantity. They included: tea cup and saucer, 6", 7", and 9" plates, 8" coupe soup, 5" fruit, 6" cereal, 9" nappy, 11-1/4" platter, 13-1/4" platter, covered sugar, regular creamer, pickle, sauce boat, and 11-1/2" chop plate.

Two complete sets were available: a 32-piece set and a 53-piece set with 9" plates and a additional 13" platter. Issued January 6, 1942 and shipped from Erwin, Tennessee.

The "Colonial Garland" pattern was an exclusive Ben Franklin semi-porcelain dinnerware. Blue and saffron garland on blue line with ivory background. Handpainted designs under the glaze. Pattern No. 3200. Cup/Saucer $15-$20. Plate $20-$25.

Fortune Pattern

"Fortune" pattern was also an exclusive Ben Franklin semi-porcelain dinnerware. This pattern will be backstamped "Franklinware-U.S.A." The pieces were available in any quantity and included: tea cup and saucer, 6", 7", and 9" plates, 8" coupe soup, 5" fruit, 6" cereal, 9" nappy, 11-1/4" platter, 13" platter, covered sugar, regular creamer, pickle, sauce boat, 11" chop plate, and covered casserole.

Two complete sets were available: a standard 32-piece set and a 53-piece set with 9" plates and a 13" platter. Issued January 6, 1942 and shipped from Erwin, Tennessee.

The "Fortune" pattern No. 57X-S-264. Floral center decal with elaborate 22-karat gold stamp on border. Semi-porcelain, umber-tone body. Cup/Saucer $15-$20. Plate $20-$25.

Ivory Tableware

Anchor Hocking's "Ivory Tableware" was an ivory glass that had the color of semi-porcelain and the translucence of fine china. It was tempered by a special process that produced a combination of beauty, strength, and durability. Issued January 12, 1943.

This 16-piece Ivory dinnerware by Anchor Hocking consists of four cups and 5-5/8" saucers, four 9-1/4" dinner plates, and four 5-1/2" desserts. Individual pieces were sold to customers so they could add to their set or make replacements. Cup/Saucer $20-$25 set. Plate $25-$30 each. Dessert $10-$12 each.

Harlequin

Manufactured by the Homer Laughlin China Company of East Liverpool, Ohio, Harlequin china was designed by Frederick Hurten Rhead and sold exclusively by F.W. Woolworth Company stores. It is one of the most popular collectible patterns today. Not promoted until 1938-1964, this ever growing popular china was first offered in four brilliant colors which were selected just for the Harlequin line: yellow, spruce green, red (maroon), and mauve blue remain the most popular collectible colors. Other colors were added over the years, including red (often referred to as tangerine), rose, turquoise, and light green. By the 1950s new colors were introduced, such as chartreuse, dark green, and gray. The last new color introduced in 1959 was medium green and was offered with only three other colors, which had been reduced to red, turquoise, yellow, and the medium green. Shown on the following pages are the colors made available to me.

Harlequin maroon 9" nappy bowl. *Dupler Collection*. $35-$40.

Harlequin turquoise oval baker. *Dupler Collection*. $25-$30.

Harlequin turquoise handled cream soup, chartreuse oatmeal bowl; tangerine 5-1/2" fruit bowl. *Dupler Collection*. Soup $25-$30. Oatmeal $11-$16. Fruit $8-$13.

Harlequin turquoise 1/2 lb. butter dish. *Dupler Collection.* $135-$150.

Harlequin turquoise demitasse cup and saucer. *Dupler Collection.* $65-$80 set.

Harlequin yellow demitasse cup and saucer. *Dupler Collection.* $68-$80 set.

29

Harlequin tangerine sauce boat. *Dupler Collection.* $25-$30.

Harlequin chartreuse sauce boat. *Dupler Collection.* $30-$35.

Harlequin tangerine sugar with lid and creamer. *Dupler Collection.* Sugar/Lid $20-$25. Creamer $15-$20.

Harlequin chartreuse creamer. *Dupler Collection.* $25-$30.

Harlequin individual creamers. *Dupler Collection.* $20-$25 each.

Harlequin basket weave nut dishes. *Dupler Collection.* $15-$20 each.

Harlequin basket weave ashtrays. *Dupler Collection.* $45-$50 each.

Harlequin tangerine saucer ashtray. *Dupler Collection.* $55-$65.

Harlequin light green regular ashtray. *Dupler Collection.* $45-$55.

Harlequin turquoise regular ashtray. *Dupler Collection.*
$44-$55.

Harlequin spruce green candleholders. *Dupler Collection.*
$200-$250 pair.

Harlequin single egg cups. *Dupler Collection.*
$20-$25 each.

Harlequin double egg cups. *Dupler Collection.* $25-$30 each.

Harlequin salt and pepper shakers. *Dupler Collection.* $15-$20 pair.

Harlequin novelty creamers. *Dupler Collection.* $25-$30 each.

Harlequin gray 22 oz. jug. *Dupler Collection.* $45-$55.

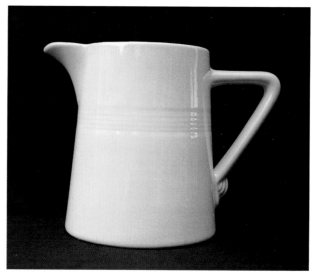

Harlequin yellow 22 oz. jug. *Dupler Collection.* $45-$55.

Harlequin tumblers. *Dupler Collection.* $45-$55 each.

35

Harlequin chartreuse service water pitcher. *Dupler Collection*. $90-$100.

Harlequin yellow teapot. *Dupler Collection*. $75-$100.

Harlequin tangerine teapot. *Dupler Collection.* $100-$125.

Harlequin rose teapot. *Dupler Collection.* $100-$125.

Harlequin gray casserole. *Dupler Collection.* $100-$125.

In 1979, Harlequin dinnerware was reissued for the 100th anniversary of the F.W. Woolworth Company. Shown above are a medium green dinner plate, turquoise salad plate, coral soup/cereal bowl, turquoise creamer, yellow sugar and yellow cup and saucer. *Dupler Collection.* Dinner plate $15-$20. Salad plate $10-$15. Soup/cereal bowl $10-$15. Creamer $10-$15. Sugar $15-$20. Cup/Saucer $10-$15.

Harlequin reissued yellow and coral round platters. *Dupler Collection.* $40-$50 each.

Harlequin reissued medium green round vegetable bowls. *Dupler Collection.* $40-$50 each.

Riviera

Riviera was a line of china produced by the Homer Laughlin China Co. in 1938 and made exclusively for the G.C. Murphy Co.

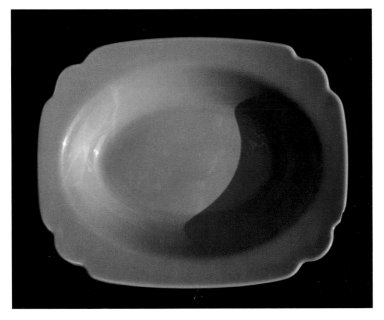

Riviera mauve blue 9" curved sides oval baker. *Dupler Collection.* $30-$35.

Riviera 7" and 6" light green plates. *Dupler Collection.* $10-$14 each.

Riviera 9" yellow and red plates. *Dupler Collection.* $15-$20 each.

Rhythm

Rhythm was another line of china produced by the Homer Laughlin China Co. It was manufactured for both the F.W. Woolworth Co. and J.J. Newberry. Circa 1951-1958. Rhythm was offered in yellow, chartreuse, gray, forest green, and burgundy.

Rhythm yellow cup and saucer. *Dupler Collection.* $8-$10 set.

Rhythm chartreuse sugar and creamer. *Dupler Collection*. Sugar $8-$10. Creamer $6-$8.

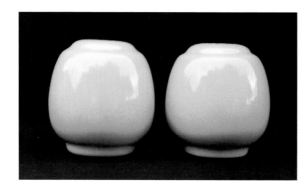

Rhythm yellow salt and pepper shakers. *Dupler Collection*. $8-$10 pair.

Rhythm 10" yellow, 9" forest green, and 7" gray plates, two 5-1/2" fruit bowls in chartreuse and burgundy, forest green sauce boat. *Dupler Collection.* 10" Plate $12-$15. 9" Plate $6-$8. 7" Plate $4-$5. Fruit bowls $4-$5 each. Sauce boat $8-$10.

Tango

Sold through the Newberry and McLellan Company stores, Tango was introduced in the late 1930s. Photograph not available.

Virginia Rose

The Virginia Rose shape was designed by Frederick Hurten Rhead and manufactured by the Homer Laughlin China Co., East Liverpool, Ohio. This popular china, reported in many decals and manufactured from 1932 through 1965, was distributed through numerous sources.

The china shown here is most often referred to as Virginia Rose "Moss Rose" or "Pinks" and was sold exclusive through the J.J. Newberry Company.

Oval 8-1/2" vegetable bowl. *Dupler Collection.* $15-$20.

Cup and saucer shown above with an 8-1/2" vegetable bowl. *Dupler Collection.* Cup/Saucer $12-$15 set. Bowl $15-$20.

10-1/2", 9-1/2", and 7" plates. *Dupler Collection.* 10-1/2" Plate $18-$20. 9-1/2" Plate $10-$20. 7" Plate $7-$10.

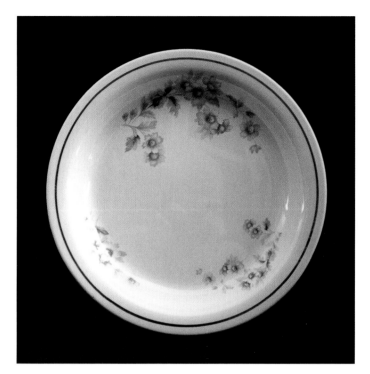

Pie baker. *Dupler Collection.* $35-$40.

Sauce boat liner (plate), 11-1/2" and 10-1/2" platters. *Dupler Collection.* Liner $20-$25. 11-1/2" Platter $20-$25. 10-1/2" Platter $15-$20.

This oval 8-1/2" vegetable bowl was an F.W. Woolworth exclusive. The "W" in front of the number on the back indicates Woolworth. *Dupler Collection.* $30-$35.

Coffee and Cookware

No. 3002-14—2 CUP
DRIP COFFEE MAKER

No. 3004-14—4 CUP
DRIP COFFEE MAKER

No. 3014-14—4 CUP
No. 3016-14—6 CUP
No. 3018-14—8 CUP
DRIP COFFEE
MAKER SETS

No. 3006-14—6 CUP
DRIP COFFEE MAKER

No. 3008-14—8 CUP
DRIP COFFEE MAKER

Original "Early Colonial" Drip Coffee Makers advertisement. Issued August 11, 1942, these coffee makers were made of vitrified china in an ivory tint with pastel decorations. They are readily available at most antique shops, flea markets, and antique shows and are presently moderately priced. Check for any hidden damage or replacement of original lid. Original labels increase the selling price. The drip coffee makers shown were available in 2-4-6- and 8-cup. The set included a matching sugar and creamer available with either the 4-6- or 8-cup coffee makers. Coffee maker $35-$40. Cream/Sugar $20-$25 set.

"All-American Aluminum" was issued August 5, 1940. The pieces shown in this original advertisement include: (A) 4-1/2 qt. Tea Kettle. Retailed at 79¢. (B) 6-qt. Covered Kettle or Pot (B-2). Retailed at 69¢/79¢. (C) 2-qt. Double Boiler. Retailed at 59¢/69¢. (D) 4-qt. Covered Sauce Pan. Retailed at 59¢/69¢. (E) 6-cup Percolator. Retailed at 50¢/59¢. (F) 8-cup Percolator. Retailed at 59¢/69¢. (G) 3-qt. French Fryer with basket. Retailed at 59¢/69¢. (H) 10-qt. Dish Pan. Retailed at 59¢/69¢. (I) 3-piece Sauce Pan Set. Retailed at 50¢/59¢ each. (J) 2-qt. 5-in-1 Combination Pan. Retailed at 69¢/79¢. (K) 14 x 10 x 2" Baking and Roasting Pan. Retailed at 50¢/59¢. (L) 2-qt. Whistling Tea Kettle. Retailed at 59¢. A "FREE Attractive Window Banner" was shipped with order of seven dozen. $15-$18 each piece.

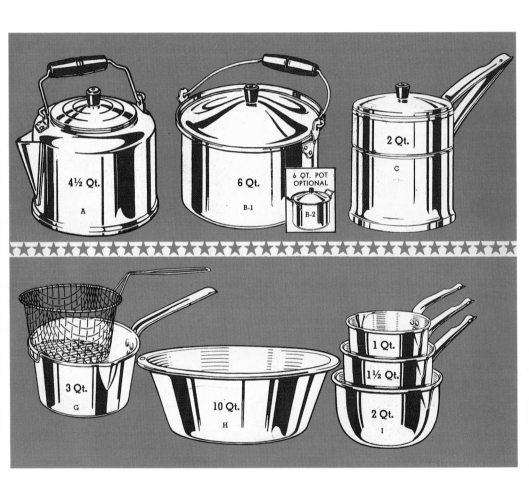

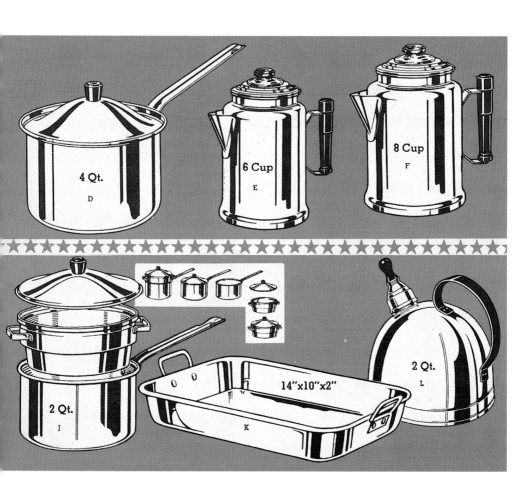

4 Qt.

D

6 Cup

E

8 Cup

F

2 Qt.

J

14"x10"x2"

K

2 Qt.

L

This original advertisement appeared in a national magazine dated May, 1944. Mirro aluminum ware was billed as the "World's Largest Manufacturer of Aluminum Cooking Utensils" and was popular at department, hardware, and home furnishing stores. *Davis Collection.* Mirro Percolator $15-$20 each.

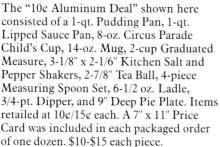

The "10¢ Aluminum Deal" shown here consisted of a 1-qt. Pudding Pan, 1-qt. Lipped Sauce Pan, 8-oz. Circus Parade Child's Cup, 14-oz. Mug, 2-cup Graduated Measure, 3-1/8" x 2-1/6" Kitchen Salt and Pepper Shakers, 2-7/8" Tea Ball, 4-piece Measuring Spoon Set, 6-1/2 oz. Ladle, 3/4-pt. Dipper, and 9" Deep Pie Plate. Items retailed at 10¢/15¢ each. A 7" x 11" Price Card was included in each packaged order of one dozen. $10-$15 each piece.

The "25¢ Aluminum Deal" shown here consisted of a 3-qt. Lipped Sauce Pan, 2-qt. Covered Pan, 1-3/8-qt. Ring Mold, 8-3/4" Colander, 9-3/8" Tube Cake Pan, and 11-1/4 x 7-1/2 x 1-1/2" Baking and Roasting Pan. A 7" x 11" Price Card was included in each packaged order of 1/2 dozen. $10-$15 each piece.

Out of the War...

New, Improved Porcelain on Steel ENAMELEDWARE!

So Colorful, So Easy to Clean AND
WITH MORE DURABILITY THAN EVER BEFORE!

Do you know what brides are getting for their shining new kitchens? What new mothers are insisting on? What thousands and thousands of women are seeking whenever *any* kitchen utensil needs replacing?

It's the wonderful, new IMPROVED Porcelain on Steel Enameledware which has only now been put on the market, after four years of intensive research. It's an amazingly improved Enameledware, with all the beauty of porcelain enamel . . . plus greater durability than ever!

This modern, research-*proved* enameledware has withstood heat tests, shock tests, and food acid tests far more severe than the normal careful use it will receive in your kitchen. The colorful, mirror-smooth, swish-clean surfaces are so stain-resistant, it's like cooking with *new* equipment all the time! With such quality, their value is unsurpassed in every price range.

Here's your assurance! Each piece of this improved Porcelain on Steel Enameledware bears the RED SEAL you see below, certifying that it meets exacting durability standards. Watch for it!

Look for the Seal . . .
YOUR ASSURANCE OF QUALITY
Manufactured by:

The Belmont Stamping and
Enameling Co.
The Canton Stamping and
Enameling Co.
Columbian Enameling and
Stamping Co., Inc.
Federal Enameling and Stpg. Co.
The Fletcher Enamel Company
The Jones Metal Products Co.
Crunden Martin Manufacturing Co.

Lisk-Savory Corp.
The Moore Enameling and
Manufacturing Co.
National Enameling & Stamp-
ing Company
The Republic Stamping &
Enameling Co.
The Strong Manufacturing Co.
United States Stamping Co.

OFFICIAL REGISTERED SEAL
New Improved
Porcelain on Steel ENAMELEDWARE
YOUR ASSURANCE OF QUALITY
ENAMELED UTENSIL MFRS.,
ADVERTISING GROUP

Modern Design Utensils for
Homes, Restaurants,
Hospitals, Institutions

Opposite page:
This advertisement for porcelain on steel enameled ware appeared in April, 1945. Enameled ware was the most modern kitchen utensil of its day and was available at most five-and-ten stores. *Davis Collection*. $20-$25 each piece. With original red seal add additional $5.00 each piece.

food won't <u>stick</u>... won't <u>burn</u> in **Wagner**

cast iron skillets

• Browns food beautifully. Gives a flavor and taste that can't be beat in any other utensil. The favorite fry pan in most homes for 59 years. It's modern cast iron, ready to use on all ranges, including electric. Get at least ONE Wagner Skillet— prove its value. 5 popular sizes, from 75c up, at 21,000 hardware—chain and department stores.

Guaranteed by Good Housekeeping

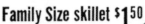
Family Size skillet $**1**50

If you can't find this 10½" family size skillet near you send $1.50 ($1.85 west of Rockies) to —

Wagner Manufacturing Co.
Dept. S, Sidney, Ohio

Wagner cast iron skillets were available in five sizes and sold at hardware, chain, and department stores. This 10-1/2" skillet sold for $1.50 in 1950. Skillet $40-$50.

Accessories

Kitchen tray, 17-1/2" x 12-3/4", decorated with pink/black flowers with matching 4-piece round canister set. There may have been a wastebasket available; the owner of these pieces has seen the dust pan. *Dupler Collection.* Tray $15-$20. Canister set $25-$35. Dust pan $20-$25. Wastebasket $35-$40.

Palatial was a new pattern in lithographed kitchenware, issued May 20, 1941. It was available in red, blue, or green and included all of the items that were in the greatest demand for use in the kitchen. The inside lining, cover, and trim of Palatial kitchenware was finished in a darker shade to give a rich appearance. This kitchenware looked like a much higher priced line and was a line five-and-ten cent stores were proud to offer their customers. This original advertisement shows Palatial kitchenware items in red: No. 83X-100, 20-3/8" high Round Basket. 13-1/2" dia.; 40-qt. capacity. Retailed at $1.00/$1.19. No. 83X-95, 13-1/2" high Round Basket. 14-1/2" dia., 26-qt. capacity. Retailed at 59¢. No. 83X88, 11-1/4" high Oval Basket. 11-1/2" long, 8-1/4" wide; 12-qt. capacity. Retailed at 25¢/29¢. No. 83X-90, Step-On-Can. Enameled insets, 7-1/2 qt. capacity. Also available in 10-qt. capacity, listed as No. 83X-91. Retailed at 69¢ (7-1/2 qt.), 69¢/79¢ (10-qt.). No. 83X-101, 1-loaf Bread Box. 12" x 5-1/4" x 5-1/2", round corners, ventilation holes. Retailed at 25¢/29¢. No. 83X-81, Large Bread Box. 13-1/2" x 9-1/2" x 8-1/4", round corners, ventilation holes. Retailed at 50¢/59¢. No. 83X-82, 4-piece Canister Set. Retailed at 59¢. No. 83X-96, 19" Canapé Trays. Retailed at 59¢/69¢. No. 83X-103, "Palatial 8-piece Kitchen Set (includes items from above listing: 4-piece Canister Set, 1 large Bread Box, 1 Oval Waste Basket, and 1 10-qt. Step-On-Can plus 1 Covered Dust Pan) Retailed at $1.60 complete set. (88) $15-$20 (95) $30-$35 (101) $20-$25 (82) $30-$35 set. (100) $40-$50 (90) $35-$40 (81) $20-$25 (96) $10-$15.

"Cross Stitch," a red and white design in matched kitchen accessories, was issued November 11, 1941. (A) Flour Sifter. 5-1/4" x 6-1/2", four wire agitators, metal handle, red wood knob, white outside, plain tin inside. Retailed at 29¢. (B) Cake Safe. 10" x 4-1/8" cover, bright tin-plate inside cover, red knob. 10-3/4" x 1/2", grooved tin tray with red border. Retailed at 49¢. (C) Flour Bin. 8-1/4" x 11-1/2", holds 14 lbs., tight fitting cover, bright tin inside. Retailed at 35¢/39¢. (D) Oval Waste Basket. 11-1/4" x 8" x 11-1/2", red inside. Retailed for 29¢. (E) Canister Set. Four round canisters, tight fitting deep covers. Retailed at 39¢/49¢. (F) Covered Dust Pan. 11-3/4" x 8-1/2", 4-1/8" red handle, black rubber edge. Retailed at 15¢. (G - H) Salt and Pepper Shakers. 2-7/16" x 3-3/8", notched and perforated cover. Retailed at 5¢ each. (J) Match Box. 3-1/2" x 3-1/4" x 6-1/4", holds one large box of matches, hole for hanging. Retailed at 10¢. (K) Soap Chip Dispenser. 4" x 4-7/8", notched cover, slotted. Retailed at 10¢. (L) Step-On Trash Can. 10 qt. inset. 8-5/8" x 10-1/4", grey lacquered finish on steel inset, heavy wire bail, pedal device raises red cover. Retailed at 69¢. (M) Bread Box. 15-3/4" x 9-1/2" x 6-5/8", large hinged lift cover, latch, red wood knob, rounded corners, bright tin-plate inside, holes for ventilation. Retailed at 59¢/69¢. (N) Serving Tray. 17-1/4" x 12-5/8" x 15/16", wide red edge for easy carrying, alcohol resisting finish. Retailed at 29¢. (P) Cocktail Tray. 14-1/4" x 9" x 3/4", wide red edge for easy carrying, alcohol resisting finish. Retailed at 10¢/15¢. (A) $15-$20 (B) $25-$30 (C) $20-$25 (D) $35-$40 (E) $30-$35 (F) $20-$25 (G-H) $10-$12 set (J) $25-$30 (K) $35-$40 (L) $40-$50 (M) $30-$35 (N) $10-$15 (P) $7-$12.

83X-84

83X-99

83X-83

83X-94

83X-89

83X-92

83X-93

83X-98

83X-97

Palatial kitchenware in blue was matched in complete ensembles by "Columbus" Blenback Oil Cloth. No. 83X-84, 4-piece Range Set. 4" x 2-1/2", Salt, pepper, sugar, and flour. Retailed at 49¢/50¢. No. 83X-99, 5-cup Flour Sifter. Removable agitator with nut lock. No. 83X-83, 11" Cake Cover and Tray, 4-3/4" deep, with knob. Retailed at 39¢/49¢. No. 83X-94, 81/2" Cookie Tin. 3-1/4" deep, holds 5 lbs. candy or cookies. Retailed at 25¢/29¢. No. 83X-89, Covered Dust Pan. 12" x 12-1/2", rubber edge. Retailed at 15¢. No. 83X-98, 31" High Chair. Four rung, 11-1/4". Retailed at $1.19/ $1.29. No. 83X-92 Match Box. 6" x 3", standard size. Retailed at 15¢. No. 83X-93, Soap Chip Dispenser. 6" x 3-3/4". Retailed at 15¢. No. 83X-97, 3-compartment Vegetable Bin. 20-1/2" x 8" x 15". Retailed at $1.19. (84) $20-$25 set. (83) $15-$20 (94) $15-$20 (98) $65-$75 (99) $15-$20 (89) $15-$20 (92) $20-$25 (93) $30-$35 (97) $60-$70.

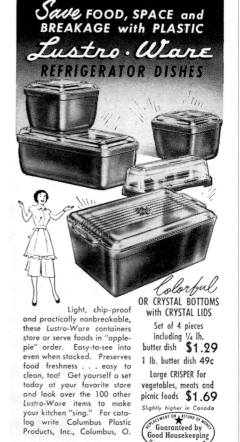

This Lustro-Ware bread box sold for $4.95 in 1951. It was manufactured by Columbus Plastic Products Inc., Columbus, Ohio and available at most stores. Over one hundred other Lustro-Ware plastic housewares items were available in matching colors. Bread Box $20-$25.

Lustro-Ware refrigerator dishes were available in 1952 at most stores. $30-$35 complete set.

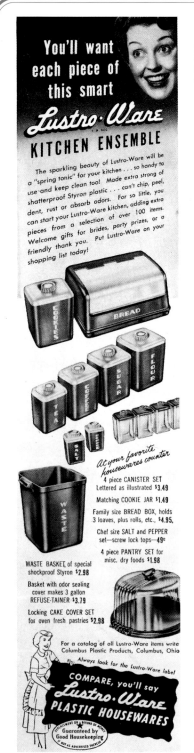

Lustro-Ware kitchen ensemble, also available in 1952. Canister set $15-$20. Cookie Jar $10-$15. Bread Box $15-$20. Salt/Pepper $5-$10 set. Pantry Set $15-$20. Wastebasket $10-$15. Cake Set $15-$20.

You'll want each piece of this smart

Lustro·Ware KITCHEN ENSEMBLE

The sparkling beauty of Lustro-Ware will be a "spring tonic" for your kitchen . . . so handy to use and keep clean too! Made extra strong of shatterproof Styron plastic . . . can't chip, peel, dent, rust or absorb odors. For so little, you can start your Lustro-Ware kitchen, adding extra pieces from a selection of over 100 items. Welcome gifts for brides, party prizes, or a friendly thank you. Put Lustro-Ware on your shopping list today!

At your favorite housewares counter

4 piece CANISTER SET
Lettered as illustrated $3.49

Matching COOKIE JAR $1.49

Family size BREAD BOX, holds 3 loaves, plus rolls, etc., $4.95.

Chef size SALT and PEPPER set—screw lock tops—49c

4 piece PANTRY SET for misc. dry foods $1.98

WASTE BASKET of special shockproof Styron $2.98

Basket with odor sealing cover makes 3 gallon REFUSE-TAINER $3.79

Locking CAKE COVER SET for oven fresh pastries $2.98

For a catalog of all Lustro-Ware items write Columbus Plastic Products, Columbus, Ohio

Always look for the Lustro-Ware label

COMPARE, you'll say
Lustro·Ware PLASTIC HOUSEWARES

Guaranteed by Good Housekeeping
IT NOT AS ADVERTISED THEREIN

colorful PLAS-TEX "LONG JOHNS" and matching Pitcher

No Metallic Taste!

"Long John" Tumblers Set of Six - $3 in Gift Box

2½ Quart Pitcher $1.95

Add festive color to dining with Plas-Tex "Long John" Tumblers. Each "Long John" holds 20 full ounces of tall cool, summertime refreshment. These thick-walled plastic tumblers keep drinks cool longer and leave no moisture "rings". The Plas-Tex Pitcher is of matching modern design. 2½ qt. capacity. In coral, teal blue, forest green, burgundy, chartreuse and grey. Available at better stores everywhere.

Perfect for TALL cool drinks

REPLACEMENT OR A REFUND OF MONEY
Guaranteed by Good Housekeeping
IF NOT AS ADVERTISED THEREIN

PLAS-TEX

MODERNIZE YOUR KITCHEN! Send today for FREE color folder

THE PLAS-TEX CORPORATION
2525 Military Ave., Los Angeles 64, Calif.
Please send me free color folder, "Modern Kitchen Helpers," showing your complete plastic housewares line.

NAME_____
STREET_____
CITY_____STATE_____

This original advertisement for Plas-Tex "Long Johns" and matching 2-1/2 qt. pitcher appeared in a national magazine dated August, 1952. The set was available at leading stores or by sending in the detachable coupon portion from the ad. $25-$30 complete set.

The collection of inexpensive colorful plastic housewares shown in this undated advertisement were "Made of Styron" and available at Ben Franklin, Butler Brothers, Scott, and "thousands of other independent variety stores." $8-10 each.

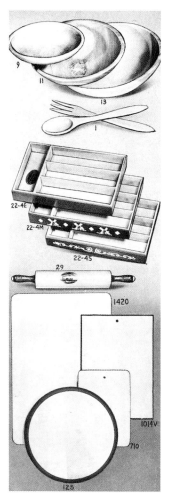

The kitchen accessories shown here were made of Vermont hardwood, issued July 28, 1942, and shipped from a factory in Stowe, Vermont. Items No. 9, 11 and 13, wooden waxed finished bowls, available in 9", 11", and 13" diameter. $7-$9 set of three. Item No. 1, fork and spoon set in waxed finish. $10-$12 set. $3-$5 pair. Below the fork and spoon set are kitchen storage containers for silverware, 13-1/2" x 8-1/2" x 2" with a clear lacquer finish inside and a enameled finish outside, four sections and mortise corners. Item No. 22-4E was available in green or red. Item No. 22-4M Dutch design came in green or red. Item No. 22-4S was a scroll design in green or red. $7-$10 each. Item No. 29, waxed rolling pin with enameled revolving handles, available with either green or red handle. $10-$12 each. Item No. 1420, 20" x 14" x 3/4" pastry board. $8-$12. Item No. 1014V, 14" x 10" x 5/16" cutting board available with either green or red edge. Item No. 710, 10" x 7" x 1/2" cutting board available with either green or red edge. Item No. 125, 12-3/4" round cake board with enameled edges in green or red. $10-$12 each.

Popular kitchen dripless servers. Manufacturer unknown. *Dupler Collection.* $8-$12 each.

Salt and Pepper Shakers

Salt and pepper shakers were readily available at the local five-and-ten-cent-stores. I am presenting a small sampling based on those made available to me, as it is impossible within the scope of this book to provide a complete illustration of the many different shakers. Shakers that were part of dinnerware or accessory sets are shown in those respective sections.

For further study of salt and pepper shakers, Schiffer Publishing Ltd. offers several reference publications that focus on collectible shakers, including *The Complete Salt and Pepper Shaker Book* by Mike Schneider, *Collecting Salt and Pepper Shaker Series* and *The Big Book of Salt and Pepper Shaker Series* by Irene Thornburg, and five volumes (*1001 Salt and Pepper Shakers* to *1005 Salt and Pepper Shakers*) by Larry Carey and Sylvia Tompkins. These comprehensive publications focus on company history, measurements, markings, paper labels, design variations, theme characters, and nodders.

No. 578
© By Permission of King Features Syndicate, Inc., 1942

No. 577
© By Permission of Famous Artists Syndicate 1942

No. 576
© By Permission of Famous Artists Syndicate 1942

No. 575
© By Permission of Famous Artists Syndicate 1942

No. 578, Barney Google and Snuffy Smith, 2-3/4" high. No. 577, Dick Tracy and Junior, 2-3/4" high. No. 576, Moon Mullins and Kayo, 2-3/4" high. No. 575 Orphan Annie and Sandy, 2-3/4" high. No. 578, $175-$200 pair. No. 577, $175-$185 pair. No. 576, $150-$175 pair. No. 575, $200-$250 pair.

The salt and pepper shakers shown here and in the next three advertisements were hand decorated, made of a plastic composition and promoted as "NEW! DIFFERENT!" Issued September 29, 1942, each pair came complete with corks and was packed in an attractive window box. An open-faced display carton was provided in which the individual boxes could be displayed. The name of a town or resort could be imprinted free on the shakers upon request. No. 500, Chipmunks, 2-1/8" high. No. 501, Corn, 2-1/2" high. No. 502, Liza and Mose, 2-3/4" high. No. 507, Traveling Bag, 1-1/2" high. No. 508, Mr. and Mrs. Santa Claus, 2-3/4" high, No. 509, Cub Bear, 2-1/4" high. No. 510, Twin Bear, 1-3/4" high. No. 511, Squirrel, 2" high. $35-$40 each set. Liza and Mose $200-$250 set.

No. 512, Outhouse, 2" high. No. 513, Victory Bombs, 2-1/2" high. No. 514, Adobe Hut, 1-3/4" high. No. 515, Indian Chief and Squaw, 2-1/2" high. No. 516, Tom, 1-7/8" high. No. 520, Red Devil, 2-1/2" high. No. 521 Snake, 2" high. No. 522, Dog Fireplug, 2-1/4" high. $35-$40 each set.

No. 523, Log Cabin, 1-1/2" high. No. 524, Cactus, 2-1/2" high. No. 524N Cactus, 2-/12" high. No. 525, Pine Cone, 1-3/4" high. No. 526 Horse Head, 2" high. No. 527 Dog Around Stump, 1-3/4" high. No. 528, Covered Wagon, 1-7/8" high. $25-$30 each.

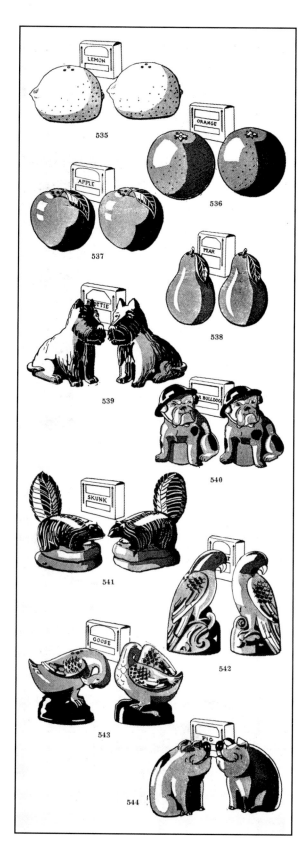

No. 535, Lemon, 1-1/2" high.
No. 536, Orange, 1-3/4" high.
No. 537, Apple, 1-3/4" high. No.
538, Pear, 2-1/4" high. No. 539
Scottie, 2-1/4" high. No 540,
Soldier Bulldog, 2" high. No.
541, Skunk, 2-1/2" high. No.
542, Parrot, 3" high. No. 543,
Goose, 2-1/4" high. No. 544,
Laughing Pig, 2-1/2". $25-$35
each set. Scottie $150-$175 set.

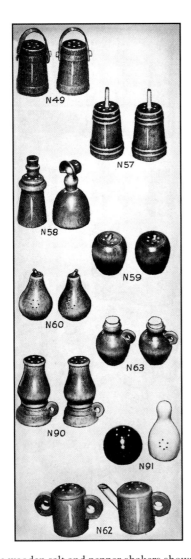

This advertisement for a "Salt'n Pepper Range Set with Plastic Tray" appeared in a 1942 magazine. $20-$25 complete.

The wooden salt and pepper shakers shown in this advertisement were issued April 21, 1942 and shipped to stores from factory No. 32, Norway, Maine. These maple and red finish novelties were a fast seller during the holidays. Issued does not necessarily mean the date of introduction or manufacture, but rather the date the paperwork was issued to the stores. No. N49, wood 2" bucket set. No. N57, wood 3-1/2" churn set. No. N58, wood 3-1/2" man and woman set. No. N59, wood 2" apple set. No. N60, wood 2" pear set. No. N63, wood 2-1/2" jug set. No. N90, wood 3" hurricane lamp set. No. N91, wood bowling set, with 2-1/2" maple finish wood pin and 1-1/2" black wood ball. No. N62, wood 2" sugar and creamer set in red finish. $10-$12 each set.

This original advertisement for Airko Free-Flow shakers appeared in the August, 1952 issue of *Ladies' Home Journal.* Airko billed itself as the "World's Largest Exclusive Shaker Manufacturer." $20-25 set.

Cookie Jars

The cookie jars and art pottery shown below were exclusively Ben Franklin items. This merchandise was available from Butler Brothers and shipped from the McCoy Pottery Company of Zanesville, Ohio.

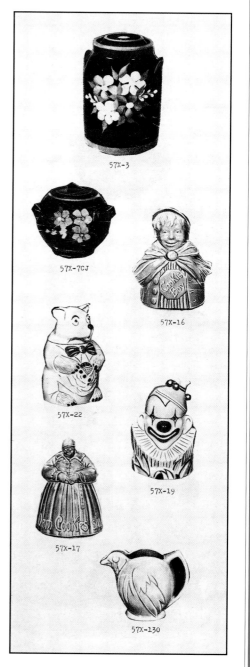

These cookie jars and art pottery were issued in April, 1943. Advertisement shows No. 57X-3, hand decorated floral design, with two handles, gloss finish. Colors available: black, yellow, green, matt white. Retailed at 59¢. $40-$50 each. No. 57X-7CJ, Hand decorated floral design, gloss finish. Colors available: black, yellow, green, blue. Retailed at 59¢. $35-$40 each. No. 57X-16, Cookie Boy design, 11-1/2", gloss finish. Colors available: white, yellow, green. Retailed at $1/$1.19. $120-$125 (White). $145-$150 (Yellow/Green). No. 57X-22, Teddy Bear cookie jar. White with colored decorations. Retailed at $1.99. $125-$130. No. 57X-19, Clown cookie jar. White with decorated face and hat, 10-1/2". Retailed at $1.59. $70-$75. No. 57X-17, Mammy cookie jar (one of the most sought after cookie jars, a Ben Franklin exclusive). "Dem Cookies shor........" can be seen on the lower portion of her skirt. Could this be the highly sought "Dem Cookies Shor Am Good" cookie jar? Has black face, red cap with green trim. Retailed at $1.59. Many collectors believe this cookie jar was never offered. You be the judge! Value N/A. No. 57X-130, Bird design in gloss finish. Colors available: white, yellow, green. Retailed at 29¢. $25-$30.

McCoy Cookie Boy in white and yellow. *Photograph Courtesy Mike Schneider.* $120-$125 (White). $145-$150 (Yellow).

McCoy Teddy Bear cookie jar.
Photograph Courtesy Mike Schneider.
$125-$130.

McCoy Clown cookie jar. *Photograph Courtesy Mike Schneider.* $70-$75.

Utensils, Gadgets, and Cleaning Supplies

F.W. Woolworth Co.'s 1929 *Home Shopping Guide* (shown on page 20) provided an assortment of items that could be used in the kitchen and the pantry. Included in the listing of items selling for 5 or 10 cents were such utensils and gadgets as tea strainers, bowl strainers, handled ladles, funnels, square graters, rotary handled flour sifters, egg beaters, meat forks, cake turners, brass cup hooks, mousetraps, kitchen knives, bread knives, butcher knives, paring knives, enamel handle kitchen utensils, orange and lemon reamers, ice picks, can openers, potato mashers, household brushes, cedar oil polish, rubber gloves, metal pot cleaners, steel wool, brillo, and dust pans. Below is just a sampling of the myriad kitchen supplies available at Woolworth's and other popular dime stores.

25¢ KRESGE'S 25¢
WONDER KNIFE
Cabbage Shredder, Vegetable Slicer and Peeler
POINT REMOVES EYES and BAD SPOTS and MAKES RADISH ROSE
============ INSTRUCTIONS HOW TO USE ============

SHREDDING CABBAGE		ASPARAGUS, LIMAS AND GREEN PEAS
First cut the cabbage in half, when long shreds are desired for cole slaw simply draw it around the edge of cabbage and when short shreds are desired for soups and combination salads just draw it up from the bottom with short strokes.	THIS TOOL IS GUARANTEED FOR TWO YEARS. Can be returned to our Factory for Repair or Exchange. Devault Patent No. 2106796	Removes Coarse fibres from celery by drawing blade over fibres. On asparagus use the same principle as on celery and on fresh lima beans and green peas. This "EZ-WAY" will cut the pods right open.

Safety Blade Will Not Cut the Hand

WONDER KNIFE

Will Not Become Dull

GENERAL PEELING

Pick up knife at shoulder with thumb and forefinger—drop it into palm of the hand and close fingers—fits hand—lay blade on vegetable—make short side stroke to break peel then pull down quickly—it's self leveling and guiding. Hold at right angles to vegetables. NOT FLAT. Excellent results are obtained on potatoes, egg plant, cucumbers, apples and in fact all kinds of skinned vegetables and fruits. The blade is made of tempered steel and the more it is used the sharper it becomes.

SCOTT PROMOTIONAL SALES COMPANY
922 Monroe Street
SAGINAW,   MICHIGAN

This 5-3/4" x 7-3/4" cardboard card held a "Kresge's Wonder Knife" priced at 25¢. The original knife is missing. Instructions were provided for use of this cabbage shredder, vegetable slicer and peeler. Card only $10-$15. Card with Knife $30-$35.

Sturdy Vegetable Brush has stiff, resilient bristles of Du Pont NYLON

This handy brush cleans vegetables quickly and efficiently . . . and helps with other kitchen duties, too. For the bristles are durable Du Pont nylon. They stay fresh, firm, resilient . . . last longer . . . serve you better. And they are easy to clean.

Springy Du Pont nylon bristles never get limp or mat down. They consistently dig in and remove the stubbornest dirt. And versatile nylon bristles won't break off . . . outwear ordinary bristles . . . give exceptional service.

You can use this nylon brush to scrape plates . . . wash dishes . . . "sweep" sinks clean. Du Pont nylon bristles don't absorb odors. A simple rinse washes grit away. Or they can be sterilized by boiling. And they dry quickly.

Whenever you buy any brush, remember that

The best brushes have DU PONT NYLON BRISTLES

Better Things for Better Living . . . *Through Chemistry*

This original advertisement for a vegetable brush made with "Du Pont Nylon Bristles" appeared in a national magazine dated August, 1952. Du Pont brushes were available at leading chain stores. $3-$5.

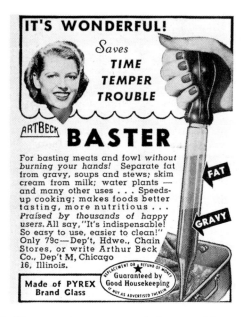

IT'S WONDERFUL!

Saves **TIME TEMPER TROUBLE**

ARTBECK **BASTER**

For basting meats and fowl *without burning your hands!* Separate fat from gravy, soups and stews; skim cream from milk; water plants — and many other uses . . . Speeds-up cooking; makes foods better tasting, more nutritious . . . *Praised by thousands of happy users.* All say, "It's indispensable! So easy to use, easier to clean!" Only 79c — Dep't, Hdwe., Chain Stores, or write Arthur Beck Co., Dep't M, Chicago 16, Illinois.

Made of PYREX Brand Glass

Guaranteed by Good Housekeeping

Only 79¢ at any department or chain store, this meat baster was made of Pyrex brand glass. $12-$15 complete.

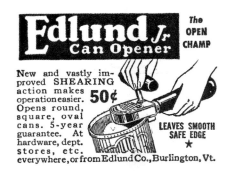

Edlund *Jr.* **Can Opener**

The OPEN CHAMP

New and vastly improved SHEARING action makes operation easier. **50¢** Opens round, square, oval cans. 5-year guarantee. At hardware, dept. stores, etc. everywhere, or from Edlund Co., Burlington, Vt.

LEAVES SMOOTH SAFE EDGE

The "Edlund Jr." can opener was available at hardware or department stores or could be ordered from the Edlund Co., Burlington, Vermont. Circa October, 1942. Opener $8-$12.

Here is an "Improved Longer Lasting Pro-Tex Burner Pad," made for "all cooking utensils." This burner pad was used directly over the burner on a kitchen stove. Retailed for 29¢. *Davis Collection*. $8-$10.

Below:
This advertisement for another Federal product, the "Big-Size Dripless Server," appeared in a June, 1943 magazine. $20-$25 complete with sticker.

This advertisement for a nut meat container-chopper-dispenser appeared in a 1941 magazine. Manufactured by Federal Tool Corp., Chicago, Illinois. $18-$20 complete with sticker.

Federal Practical Housewares were promoted at variety stores during the week of April 9-19, 1948.

BRILLO
KEEPS ALUMINUM BEAUTIFUL 10¢

BRILLO is on the job at cleaning-up time after meals. BRILLO cleans and polishes in one operation—quickly, easily, thoroughly. No biting alkalies — no harsh irritants — no messy rags — just neat lubricated metal fibre BRILLO pads and pure vegetable BRILLO polishing soap. Use BRILLO pads over and over again—10c worth cleans 140 pots and pans.

Contains 5 metal-fibre Pads and Polishing Soap. At Woolworth, Kresge, Kress, McClellan and all 10c and 25c stores, and at leading department, hardware and grocery stores. Brillo Mfg. Co., Brooklyn, N. Y.

CLEANS AND POLISHES IN ONE OPERATION

Now you SEE it

- now you DON'T

Grease disappears like magic when

BRILLO

DOES THE WORK!

IT'S the world's fastest cleanser thanks to the miracle combination of BRILLO soft metal-fibre Pads and special-formula Polishing Soap BRILLO cleans and polishes in one simple operation. It's economical, too, because BRILLO always goes further. Try BRILLO today on your hardest-to-clean pots and pans!

KEEPS ALUMINUM BRILLIANT
2 EASY WAYS

GREEN BOX
5 Pads and Soap Separate

EITHER PACKAGE 10c

RED BOX
5 Soap-Filled Pads

At Woolworth, Kresge, Kress, Grant, McCrory and all 10c and 25c stores, and at leading department, hardware and grocery stores. BRILLO Mfg. Co., Inc., Brooklyn, N. Y.
New utensil FREE should BRILLO fail to clean

Aluminum
PRECIOUS METAL
Handle with care!

BRILLO
BRIGHTENS AND PRESERVES ALUMINUM

Now, more than ever, use Brillo on your pots and pans. This double-action combination of Brillo square metal-fiber pads and polishing soap cleans like lightning; brightens and preserves your precious aluminum and all other pots and pans. Use genuine Brillo after every meal.

Only BRILLO offers 2 Easy Ways to KEEP ALUMINUM BRILLIANT

RED BOX
5 Soap-Filled Pads

GREEN BOX
5 Pads and Soap Separate

EITHER PACKAGE 10¢

At Woolworth, Kresge, Kress, Newberry, McLellan, Green, all variety stores, and leading department, hardware and grocery stores. BRILLO Manufacturing Company, Incorporated, Brooklyn, New York.

BRILLO

New utensil FREE should BRILLO fail to clean

Outside the kitchen door
THE HOLIDAY FEAST

Inside the kitchen door
GREASY POTS AND PANS

BIG MEAL DAYS ARE S.O.S DAYS

**S.O.S.
SHINES**
ALUMINUM
POTS & PANS
STOVES
BAKING GLASS
LINOLEUM
BROILERS
COFFEE POTS
NICKEL
OVER 40 USES

S.O.S
Magic
Scouring
Pads

The S.O.S Company
CHICAGO

THIS PACKAGE CONTAINS FOUR PADS

the
SOAP
is in the
PAD

.... a stacked sink
has no terrors for the
woman who scours her
pots and pans with this
magic cleaner

The feast for the family. But *for you,* the housewife, those pots and pans. Greasy, scorched, stained.

Never mind—you can have them shining again in double-quick time.

S.O.S. will do the trick. Like magic.

It "cuts" the grease. It scours away the burnt-on food. It polishes metal, glass and enamel. *In one easy, simple operation.*

Just wet the edge of an S.O.S. pad—rub—rinse—and your utensils will shine like new again.

So when you go holiday-shopping, be sure to put S.O.S. on your list. At your grocer's, hardware, department or five and ten cent store. Or mail the coupon below for a generous free trial package.

FREE
Mail this coupon or a post-card to The S.O.S. Company, 6263 W. 65th St., Chicago, Ill., and we will send you free and postpaid a generous trial package of S.O.S. You'll like it. It's wonderful!

NAME

ADDRESS_____D

This *Ladies' Home Journal* ad from November, 1934 promoted S.O.S. Scouring Pads, a competitor of Brillo. They were sold at grocery, hardware, department, or five-and-ten cent stores. *Davis Collection.* Original advertisement $15-$18.

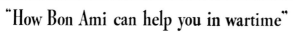

"hasn't scratched yet!"

Bon Ami "hasn't scratched yet!" according to this advertisement promoting the wartime benefits of Bon Ami cleaning supplies.

Left:
Advertisement for Bon Ami household cleanser. "Easier Cleaning for Bathtubs and Sinks." Circa 1953.

Right:
The Mirro Coffee Perk Cleaner kit included one can of cleaner, a spout brush, and stem brush. It could be used for "all types and makes of coffee makers." The original "G.C. Murphy" 69¢ price sticker is on the back of the carton. *Davis Collection.* $30-$35 complete.

Kitchen Decor

During the 1930s through the 1950s, it was not uncommon for house-wives to cover shelves and/or storage areas with attractively embossed printed paper. One manufacturer was The Royal Lace Paper Works, Inc., from Brooklyn, New York, who manufactured under the trademark Roylace Paper Goods. Roylace™ Paper Goods were of a high grade bond paper, embossed and printed, with patented double edge borders. Royledge™ shelving paper had a quality customers demanded and was available at five-and-ten cent stores, neighborhood groceries, and department stores. Issued September 30, 1941.

The Royledge™ metal counter display rack for dealers was available only in a mahogany finish with a two-color lithograph front sign. It included a half dozen each of the following shelf papers in assorted colors and patterns: Red (Teatime, Big'n Little Polk Dot, Mexicana Silhouette, Flowered Tile, Fruit, Dot'n Dash, Flower Cart, Bouquet, Daisy, Tulip, and Wot Not), Green (Quilted, Dot'n Dash, Posy, Large Rose, and Daisy), Blue (Dutch Couple, Stipple, Dot'n Dash, and Flower Cart), Yellow (Stipple and Daisy), Black (Daisy only), Red/White and Blue (Patriotic). This metal display rack was furnished free upon request with one gross of shelf paper of the store's choosing. Issued September 30, 1941. $75-$80 complete.

Royledge™ 9 foot sections of shelf paper and Royledge™ "Xtra Width" shelf lining paper plus decorative edging. Economy Package 39¢. Original S.S. Kresge's label on back. *Davis Collection.* $15-$18 each section complete.

Two original black and white Royledge™ shelving advertisements, showing the use of shelf paper to beautify the kitchen. "All my friends are copying ME!" 9 feet for 5¢, dated 1940. "Colorful Beauty For Your Kitchen," 9 feet for 6¢, dated 1942. *Keister Collection.* Advertisements $5-$8 each.

New Color for Your Kitchen !

Cut out and try these new patterns on your shelves—

See how your kitchen "sings with new color" when you glorify all shelves with new "Plasti-Chrome" Royledge. "Plasti-chrome" finish makes colors brighter, gayer than ever—transforms your kitchen with exciting color beauty! Yet new Royledge costs only about a penny a foot. Select gorgeous patterns now at 5 & 10's, Supermarkets, Housefurnishing, Naborhood, Dept. Stores.

Royal Lace Paper Works, Inc., Bklyn.
"Royledge" Td. Mk. Reg. U. S. Pat. Off.

Shelf Lining Paper & Edging all-in-one. 9 ft. & 24 ft. pkgs.

NEW ADHESIVE Edging— moisten and apply to metal & wood shelves

NEW ≋ Plasti-Chrome ≋

Royledge

new!

new!

Top photo: "Apples 'n' Dots" Royledge. Above: "Ribbon 'n' Eyelet", Below: "Paper Dolls"

Two original color Royledge shelving advertisements (left and right), showing some of the popular patterns available. "New Color for Your Kitchen," dated 1952. Royledge shelf lining paper and edging (ALL-IN-ONE), dated 1953. *Davis Collection*. Advertisements $5-$8 each.

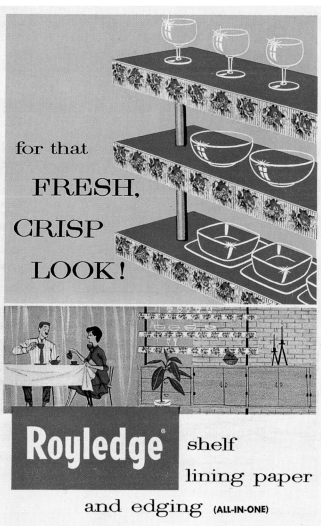

for that

FRESH, CRISP LOOK!

Royledge® shelf lining paper and edging (ALL-IN-ONE)

Fresh as a Spring rainbow...sunny and gay, new Spring Royledge patterns have just arrived— to give your kitchens and closets a new look, a new lift...for pennies! You'll love the sparkling colors, the fresh crispness, the decorator-styled patterns. And to be practical, you'll love, too, the way the Plasti-chrome surface cleans quick as a wink, never fades, never stains, and never— never—curls! Don't let another Spring day go by! Get Royledge edging and lining all-in-one; comes in standard or Xtra-width. Choose your favorite pattern now at Variety, Super Market, Department and other stores. Write for booklet telling fun-ways to decorate with Royledge. Royal Lace Paper Works, Inc., 99 Gold Street, Brooklyn 1, N. Y. (A subsidiary of Eastern Corp.)

Guaranteed by Good Housekeeping

Designed for *Royal* living, everyday!

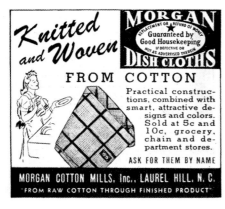

Sold at five-and-ten, grocery, chain, and department stores, "Morgan Dish Cloths" were promoted in 1943. Morgan Cotton Mills, Inc., Laurel Hill, North Carolina. Cloths in original packaging $5-$10.

1946 advertisement for "Morgan Dish Cloths," describing their features as bright, attractive, fast colors and smart designs. Cloths in original packaging $5-$10.

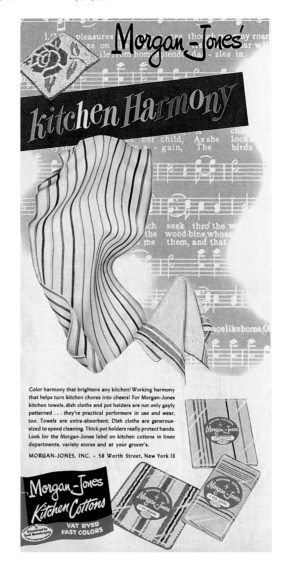

In 1952, the Morgan-Jones trademark appeared on linens available at department, variety, and grocery stores. Cloths in original packaging $5-$10.

Part II

The Home and Garden Aisles
Home Furnishings and Decor

Real values in walnut finish, unfinished occasional tables, and accessories were available in most dime stores. Unfinished furniture promoted sales in paints, varnishes, brushes, sandpaper, and glue. Dime stores stocked a variety of unfinished tables in both new and modern styles. Shown here is a group of occasional tables issued April 21, 1942. They were made of heavy hardwood, finished in walnut, and had reinforced shelves and fancy turnings. Wholesale $1.95 each. Retail $2.95 each. (A) 16" x 16" x 25-1/2" lamp table. (B) 16" x 16" x 26" drum table. (C) 14" x 14" x 26" night stand with drawer. (D) 11" x 22" x 22" book trough end table. (E) 11" x 22" x 22" half-round table. (F) 11" x 27" x 22" radio table. $75-$80 each.

DON'T BE A STATISTIC!

play it safe with *COSCO*

COSCO De Luxe Step Stool (Model 4-D): Tubular steel construction, gleaming chromium finish. Rubber-treaded, swing-away steps. All-plastic upholstery, red, black, blue, green, yellow or mother-of-pearl gray.

Guaranteed by Good Housekeeping

Get a Cosco Step Stool . . . a Comfortable Seat and a Safer Ladder . . . All In One!

Don't use that risky, makeshift ladder another day. Reach top shelves easily—do your curtain-hanging and *all* your "climbing" tasks—on a steady, sturdy, *safer* Cosco Step Stool. No household is complete without one. *Swing out* the steps and you have an all-steel, six-leg ladder—tested to support 2,000 pounds. *Swing in* the steps (or leave them out for a footrest) and you have a comfortable, smartly styled seat, 24″ high, that's perfect for preparing vegetables, ironing—doing scores of tiresome household chores in sit-down comfort. All edges are rounded or turned under to protect hands and hose. Entire stool wipes sparkling clean with a damp cloth. Don't delay, get a "famous-for-quality" Cosco Step Stool. At department, furniture or hardware stores. Model illustrated, about $16.95; others from about $9.95.

HAMILTON MANUFACTURING CORPORATION • COLUMBUS, INDIANA

Three Models—

Cosco Step Stools are built for every budget. Your choice of all-enamel or chromium-enamel finish; with or without back; all-plastic upholstery or plain; rubber-treaded steps; up to six colors. Get yours today.

For the best in quality, look for the Cosco Trademark. Accept no substitutes.

Household Stools, Chairs and Utility Tables
Sold also in Canada and South America.

In 1951, the Cosco step stools shown in this illustration sold for $16.95. Manufactured by Hamilton Manufacturing Corporation, Columbus, Indiana. Stool $75-$100 complete.

IT'S TRUE! THESE LOVELY CLOPAY CURTAINS COST ONLY 39¢

WOW! LET'S CURTAIN EVERY WINDOW FROM ATTIC TO BASEMENT!

NO WINDOW need be dull or dingy now. For kitchen, bath or bedroom—for basement, hall or attic, CLOPAY *Hollywood Style* Curtains bring gaiety and charm for just a few pennies.

Five-piece sets of genuine plasticized cellulose in brisk polka dot, gingham or strawberry patterns. Red, blue or green. They're a full 54 inches long and can be shortened just by cutting.

CLOPAY COTTAGE SETS

ONLY 59¢

So smart, so fresh—CLOPAY Cottage Sets make any window sing. 7-Piece set includes 2 top panels, 2 sash panels, 2 tiebacks, and an extra width of valance.

CLOPAY *Lintoned* DRAPES

ONLY 98¢

Charm and elegance at amazingly low cost. Stunning florals, stripes and plaids. Generous 2⅔ yards long, with matching tie-backs.

Free Booklet: "Beautiful Windows at Low Cost." Write to: Clopay Corp., 1282 Clopay Sq., Cincinnati 14, O.

CLOPAY

Reg. U. S. Pat. Off.

Beautiful windows at low cost

54 Now available at 5 and 10c Stores, Variety Stores, Department and Other Stores.

Beautiful Clopay™ curtains and drapes were available in 1947 at five-and-ten, variety, department, and other stores. $30-$40 complete sets.

Blenback for tables!
Colorful, modern patterns lend good cheer to every-day meals. This luscious fruit design (Orchard Lane, No. 5279) brightens either kitchen or dining room table, keeps its clean, fresh look week in, week out.

try these

do-it-yourself decorating ideas

from the personal scrapbook of Constance Hunter, home decorator

Now! Dozens of bright ideas for your home with colorful Blenback Oil Cloth. Practical ideas, too, because Blenback is a real work-saver. Dust and grease wipe off with a damp cloth. The coated fabric surface doesn't spot or stain, stays color-fresh, wears and wears. Go to your store this week and buy the new patterns in Blenback Oil Cloth by the yard, as individual table covers or in matching ready-made ensembles of chair backs and cushions, scarfs, edging and shelf covering.

Blenback Wastebasket Cover
Glamorize old or chipped wastebaskets, canisters, breadbox with matching fabric-base Blenback Oil Cloth. Pastes or tapes on easily, stands abuse.

Blenback Basket Liner
Makes handy laundry hamper out of ordinary bushel basket. Slips over wire handles, stays in place. Ready-made in gay patterns. Sold as Universal Clothes Basket Liners at variety stores.

Blenback Sink and Stove Splasher
Colorful protection for paint, paper, plaster walls. Grease spots wash right off. Easy to install. Just paste, tack or tape it up.

Blenback Drawer Liner
Dress up drawers with bright, new Blenback patterns. The liners take only a minute to cut. They stay put, and they dust clean in a jiffy.

FREE! "Do-it-yourself Decorating Ideas"
A book full of clever ways to make your home smarter, more colorful, more livable. Mail coupon to Columbus Coated Fabrics Corp., Dept. WD-52, Columbus 16, Ohio.

Name_____

Address_____

Town_____ State_____

Decorate doors and shelves with bright new Blenback Oil Cloth. Use it on closet walls, too. Smooth surface sheds dust. For extra smartness, also cover hat boxes in Blenback.

COLUMBUS Blenback oil cloth

By the makers of Wall-Tex fabric wall covering and Col-O-Vin vinyl plastics by the yard

In 1952, Columbus Blenback oil cloth was available in many patterns and sold by the yard at any variety store. This original advertisement shows some of the do-it-yourself ideas for using oil cloth. Manufactured by the Columbus Coated Fabrics Corp., Columbus, Ohio.

3 DESIGNS—3 COLORS

The eye-appealing waste baskets shown here and in the next advertisement were beautiful and gracefully shaped. Every piece in this assortment had what it took to be a real value at 25¢ to 29¢ retail. Issued May 20, 1941. The three baskets here feature different designs, colors, and sizes. 7-3/4" x 11-1/2", 7-1/4" x 11-1/2", and 7-1/8" x 11-1/2" with assorted Nasturtium, Clematis, and Dogwood designs. Colors; gray, ivory and blue. $40-$45 each.

BLOSSOM AND GARDEN GATE DESIGNS   **ROSE AND DOGWOOD DESIGNS**

The Blossom and Garden Gate designs shown in this advertisement retailed for 29¢/35¢. They featured 12-qt. capacity, assorted designs, assorted ivory outside, green or red inside. The Rose and Dogwood designs also retailed for 29¢/35¢. They had the same capacity and came in assorted colors: dubonnet, olive green, and midnight blue with gray inside. $40-$45 each.

Kitchen or bath wastebasket decorated with roses, buds, and green leaves is 11-1/4" high with a diameter of 7-1/2". *Dupler Collection.* $25-$30.

You can save money at every meal by using these beautiful Roylie *Lace-Paper* Place Mats! Dresses up the table—and actually costs less than mere laundering of linen. Handy new Family Pkg. contains enough place mats to serve 12 meals or more for family of 4. You'll want other sizes, shapes and patterns of Roylies also—for meals and entertaining—under glasses, desserts, hors d'oeuvres, etc. At 5 & 10's, supermarkets, nabor-hood, dept. stores.

Royal Lace Paper Works, (Inc.), Brooklyn
Trade Mark "Roylies" Reg. U. S. Pat. Off.

THIS EXQUISITE TABLE-SETTING COSTS LESS THAN MERE LAUNDERING OF LINENS

EXQUISITE · MONEY-SAVING

R*O*YLIES
Lace Paper Doylies

Original advertisement for Roylies Lace Paper Doylies, designed to "dress up the table." Sold at dime stores, supermarkets, and department stores. Manufactured by Royal Lace Paper Works, (Inc.), Brooklyn. *Keister Collection*. $8-$10 per package.

Stitch Pattern

Allover Lace Pattern

Floral Basket Pattern

5568

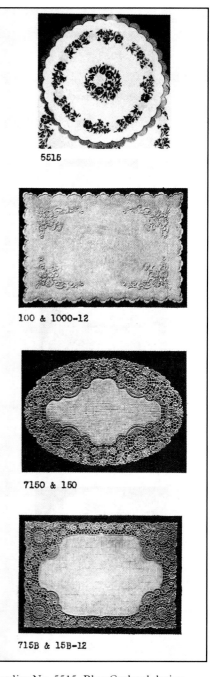

5515

100 & 1000-12

7150 & 150

715B & 15B-12

Roylies Stitch Pattern, Allover Lace Pattern, Floral Basket Pattern and No. 5568 Round Shape" 5¢ paper doilies, packaged in transparent glassine envelope. Round shape doilies were the newest and most popular patterns. $10-$12 each complete.

Roylies No. 5515, Blue Garland design doilies. Retailed for 10¢. No. 100 & 1000-12, Oblong Daisy Pattern, white linen finish. No. 7150 & 150, Oval Lace edge, solid center, white only. Roylies 10¢ placemats. No. 715B & 15B-12, Oblong lace edge, solid center, white only. $10-$12 complete.

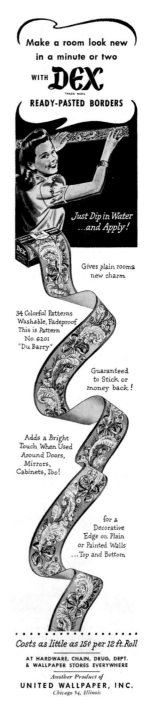

"It's easy - Just wet it and put it up!" according to this Trimz Ready-Pasted Border advertisement, dated 1943. *Keister Collection*. Border $8-$12 per package.

Another original Trimz Ready-Pasted Borders advertisement. Borders were sold at dime, department, hardware, and paint stores. *Keister Collection*. Border $8-$12 per package.

Dex was another brand of ready-pasted borders, as shown in this original Dex advertisement. United Wallpaper, Inc. Chicago 54, Illinois, April 1945. *Keister Collection*. $8-$12 per package.

Original 1946 advertisement for Meyercord decals, which sold for 10¢, 20¢ and 39¢ at department, five-and-ten, hardware, variety, paint, and chain stores. The Meyercord Co. "World's Largest Manufacturer of Decals," Chicago, Illinois; Can. Decal Co., Toronto. *Keister Collection*. $8-$12 per package.

The "Service Banners" shown here were issued January 27, 1942 and shipped from factory No. 81, Denver, Colorado. These popular patriotic motto and service banners rated a place of distinction in any home or office. "No matter what the surrounding, the easy-to-read letters and attractive colors fit. There are millions of men in service today and there are millions of persons and families vitally interested— these are your sales possibilities." No. 800 (Remember Pearl Harbor) - 850 (Service Banner), 12" x 17-1/2" white rayon, glossy satin finish. American flag with 2" blue fringe, appropriate quotations, and bright red rayon cord. No. 780 (Remember Pearl Harbor) - 790 (Service Banner), 12" x 19-1/2" blue cotton felt with flocked American flag design and 3" gold color fringe. Appropriate quotations and red, white, and blue cord. No. 800-850 $25-$30 each. No. 780-790, $40-$45 each.

In the late 1930s, an employee of the F.W. Woolworth Company, Bill Thompson, along with New York importer Max Eckardt approached the Corning Glass Company of Corning, New York about developing an American-based glass ornament business (up to this time, F.W. Woolworth, S.S. Kresge, and S.H. Kress were all importing Christmas ornaments from Germany). In 1939, the Corning Company in Wellsboro, Pennsylvania produced and shipped 235,000 blown ornaments to the F.W. Woolworth Company. In 1945, "Bubble-Lites" first became available. They were created by Carl Otis, then an employee of the Montgomery Ward Company. Otis later became associated with NOMA lites and his "Bubble-Lites" idea was perfected.

Customers began to purchase the bubbling colored liquid lights, but as Christmas came and went so did the "Bubble-Lites," as a new concept in Christmas tree lighting appeared on the market in the form of "Miniature Lights" sets.

By the 1960s, F.W. Woolworth was the only retailer continuing to sell the now famous "Bubble-Lites" and their replacement bulbs. "Bubble-Lites" have once again become the popular lighting for Christmas trees. They have escalated in price and can be somewhat hard to find.

Woolworth's glass Christmas tree ornaments. *Courtesy of Lon and Lynda Lemons.* $18-$20 complete in original carton.

Christmas Lights by NOMA. "Each lamp burns independently." This set could be connected and used with other types of sets. *Courtesy of Lon and Lynda Lemons.* $20-$25 complete in original carton.

Festive wreaths for holiday decor. No. 90-14, 15" bright red oak leaves decorated with three frosted sprays, three bunches of green pepper grass, one cluster of six white berries and four natural frosted cones. No. K29, 15" green lycopodium decorated with eight clusters of six red berries and eighteen natural frosted cones. No. K5, 15" bright red lycopodium decorated with eight clusters of six silver berries and eighteen red cones. No. 150-6, 18" frosted green lycopodium decorated with ten clusters of seven red berries, green oak leaves, and frosted red cones. No. 150-14, 18" bright red lycopodium and oak leaves decorated with green evergreen sprays, five sprays of white grasses, three clusters of eight white berries, frosted green leaves, and seven natural frosted cones. No. 150-19, 18" bright red lycopodium decorated with five frosted evergreen sprays, five bunches of white pepper grass, three clusters of eight berries, and seven large natural frosted cones. No. 198-1, 20" green lycopodium decorated with three frosted edge red cycas leaves, thirteen clusters of seven red berries, green oak leaves, eight bunches of red pepper grass, seven bunches of white pepper grass and nine clusters of large natural frosted cones. No. 198-18, 20" green lycopodium decorated with eleven clusters of nine red berries, large frosted edge red cycas leaf, four bunches of white grasses, five bunches of red pepper grass and nine large frosted red cones. No. 198-21, 20" Frosted Nile green lycopodium decorated with frosted green palm leaves, sixteen clusters of red berries and six large frosted red cones. $20-$25 complete.

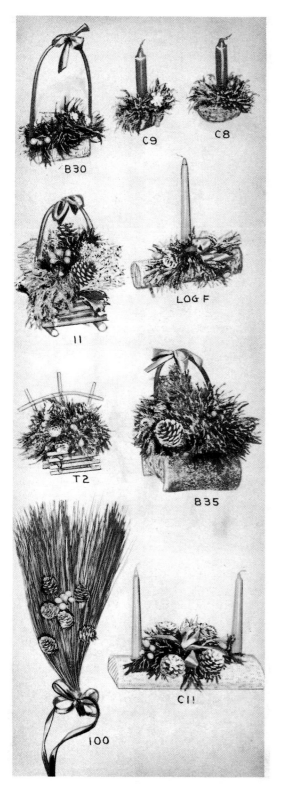

Assorted holiday decorations, issued August 4, 1942. No. B30, half birch with handle table decoration. Decorated green lycopodium, two clusters of four red berries, five natural frosted cones and red ribbon bow. No. C9 - C8, 3" birch log circles decorated with frosted green lycopodium, two red berries, one natural frosted cone, 5" red candle, cellophane wrapped. No. 11, filled cherrywood basket filled with red and green lycopodium and oak leaves, white pepper grass, one cluster of six red berries, two large natural frosted cones, red ribbon bow. No. LOGF, 7-1/2" birch log decorated with frosted green lycopodium, two clusters of red berries, red ribbon bow, 7-1/2" red candle, cellophane wrapped. No T2, 7" red trellis trimmed with frosted green lycopodium, two clusters of two red berries, and five natural cones. No. B35, filled birch log basket with frosted green lycopodium, two clusters of four red berries, red lycopodium, two large natural frosted cones, red ribbon bow. No. C11, 10" flat birch log decorated with green lycopodium, two clusters of four red berries, four natural frosted cones, red ribbon bow, and two 7-1/2" red candles. No. 100, 16" green needle grass door hanger decorated with one cluster of six red berries, six natural cones, red ribbon bow. $15-$18 each complete.

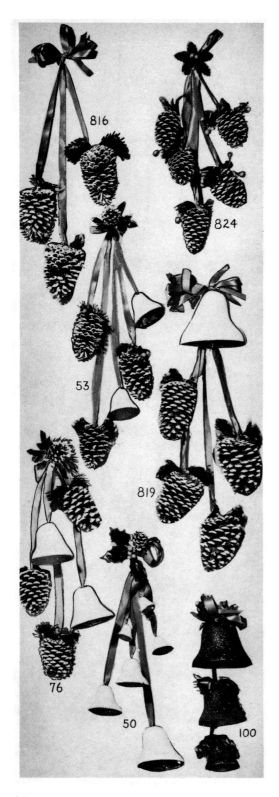

No. 816, 18" pine cone hanger with three white tipped cones on three red ribbons, princess pine with red berries tied at the top of each cone. No. 824, 17" pine cone hanger with five cones. White tipped cones on red ribbon, princess pine and red berries tied at the top of each cone, silver poinsettia with pine and berries at the top. No. 53, 20" cone and bell hanger with three cones and two white bells on red ribbon, berry and holly leaf top. No. 819, 27" cone and bell hanger with four pine cones and one 6" half bell for mounting on wall, attached to four red ribbons. No. 76, 20" cone and bell hanger with three pine cones, three bells, holly leaves, and berries. No. 50, 20" bell hanger with six graduated white bells, green holly, cones and berries on red ribbon. No. 100, 14" bell hanger with three graduated blue bells, holly leaves, and berries on red ribbon. $18-$20 each.

This Master Craft store display rack increased candle sales and was given free to any store with an initial order of $15.00 or more.

Candle selection from The Master Craft Candle Works, Kearny, New Jersey. No. 1, hand dipped tapered, available in 22", 18", 15" 12", 10" and 8" length. Also 5" length for hurricane lamps. No. 2, modern leaf design 12" taper. No. 3, formal dinner candle. No. 4, molded 7-1/2" fluted taper. No. 5, 16" flower-lite tapers, hand-dipped tapers. Seven per carton with large cellophane window. No. 6, two 9" Bayberry candles. Cellophane wrapped, packed in carton with Bayberry verse. For an additional 6¢ each carton was enclosed in an attractive blue Christmas greeting mailing container that could be mailed anywhere in the United States. No. 7, household candle, packed two to a cellophane package. Colors available: white, red, and green. No. 8, 6" spindle twist. No. 9, plumber or coach candle. No. 10, 3" x 1" stub candelabra candle. No. 11, large birthday candles. No. 12, holders for large birthday candles. No. 13, holders for small birthday candles. No. 14, small birthday candles, 36 candles per carton. No. 15, Romany decorated 12" hand-decorated taper. No. 16, 11" candy stripe twisted, molded candle. No. 17, red 15" hand-dipped candle with evergreen tree. No. 18, twisted 11". No. 19, molded 14" x 1-1/8". No. 20, twisted 14", popular all year round. No. 21, tapered 11" x 1-1/2". No. 21, Same style as No. 21, 16" x 1-1/2". No 22, sanctuary or night lights 10 and 15 hour sizes. Packed in cellophane window cartons. No. 23, candle fitters, 12 round flannel discs, packed in cellophane envelope attached to card. (makes any candle fit holder.) No. 24, Lites, package held 10 tapers 6-1/2" long. Used for lighting after-dinner smokes, gas appliances, or fireplaces. No. 25, candelabra candles 6" x 1/2". No. 26, household candle, packed four to a cellophane carton. No. 27, night light glasses in 10 and 15 hour sizes.

Hardware and Household Goods

The many hardware items sold at dime stores for home use included wood screws, nickel screws, screw hooks and eyes, screw drivers, strap and butt hinges, safety hasps, padlocks, door bolts, gate hooks and eyes, nail sets, taper and flat files, machine oilers and oil, pliers, tack hammers, carpet tacks, large size hammers, and machinists' wrenches. There were also saw handles and blades, picture wire and hangers, coat and hat hooks, cup hooks, brass head tacks, leathering tacks and furniture slides, glass knobs for dressers and cabinets, electric cords, extension cord sets, keysockets, shells and caps, pull chain sockets, key socket mechanisms, fuse plugs, carbon lamps, twin light sockets, heater plugs, flashlight batteries, bulbs and cases, victrola oilers, and corks. For painting needs, stores carried paint brushes, household paints and enamels in many colors, varnish, stains, and brushes.

For use in the garage, the five-and-ten offered cleaning cloths, hand soap, auto pliers, copper oilers, machine oil, tire tape, sponges, socket wrenches, hammers, canvas gloves, parcel post twine, metal polishes and extension electric light sets.

"Stick 'Em Up!" Selfix hooks were available at all five-and-ten, department, or hardware stores. Interested customers could also write directly to the company to determine the nearest store.

This 12" paint stick was provided "Compliments of S.S. KRESGE CO." and also advertised Flo-Mor paint. *Davis Collection.* $50-$60.

Widen those "difficult" windows
without marring walls—

Brackets attach to window casing; allow track to extend beyond wall without marring wall.

with JUDD Extending Traverse Rod

Make even the most difficult window a thing of beauty this easy way! Drapes hung on Judd Extending Traverse Rod make your windows look larger, admit more light . . . because the drape covers the wall, not the window. Drapes open or close with a pull of the draw cord. Rods are in Judd's exclusive "Walls of Troy" motif; off-white enamel on enduring steel.

JUDD PLEATMASTER®
Makes Pleated Drapes *in Minutes*

Any woman can do it with Pleatmaster Hooks and Tape: no difficult measuring, no intricate stitching. Tape available by the yard, hooks in any quantities needed, or in handy kit containing hooks and tape for a 10-pleat pair of drapes . . . at drapery departments and variety stores everywhere.

Get this new Judd book, full of ideas for modern window treatments. Send 15¢ in coin.

JUDD decorator-styled **Drapery Hardware**

H. L. JUDD COMPANY, Wallingford, Conn.
Dept. WD

PAINT BRUSHES SCARCE!
Keep NEW brushes soft
RENEW old brushes

Conserve valuable paint brushes! *Save them* by using DIC-A-DOO PAINT BRUSH BATH after every use. Amazingly efficient in loosening, washing away paint from bristles. Brush remains good as new for long time. Restores old hardened brushes to usefulness. Enough to clean several brushes. Costs only 5 cents. Get it at hardware or 5-&-10¢ stores. You'll want to keep several packages on hand. The Patent Cereals Co., Makers of DIC-A-DOO Paint Cleaner, Geneva, N.Y.

DIC-A-DOO Brush Bath

Advertisement for "Dic-A-Doo Paint Brush Bath." $18-$20 original packaged bath.

Original advertisement from April, 1952 for Judd Drapery Hardware, sold "at drapery departments and variety stores everywhere."

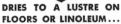

For longer, quieter, trouble-free operation, lubricate vacuum cleaners, washing machines, electric refrigerators periodically with Heavy Body 3-IN-ONE Oil. Get it at Hdwe, Drug, Grocery, 10¢ Stores.

An original 1942 advertisement for "3-In-One Heavy Body Oil" in metal container. $15-$18 original container.

An original 1943 advertisement for "3-In-One Heavy Body Oil" in glass bottle. $15-$18 original bottle.

"Better Home Care Made Easier." These products, available at "All Dealers and 10¢ Stores," included Old English Liquid Wax, Black Flag Insect Spray, 3-In-One-Oil, Plastic Wood and Antrol Ant Killer. Circa 1941. Products $18-$25 each.

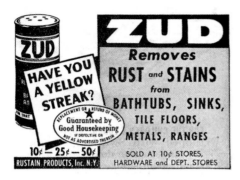

"Zud" removed rust and stains and carried the famous "Good Housekeeping" guarantee. Rustain Products, Inc., N.Y. $10-$12 original container.

Astonishing new Furniture Polish makes scratches vanish like MAGIC!

Tables, chairs, beds, radio cabinets, bureaus—*all* your furniture in *every* room—just touch them up with "Old English Scratch Removing Polish," and see a *double miracle* performed before your astonished eyes!

Old-looking, dull, dingy pieces, sparkle and shine like new. And as you polish, ugly scratches amazingly disappear.

Get Old English Scratch Removing Polish at grocery, hardware, drug, department and 10¢ stores. Only 25¢ a bottle—and the beauty it brings is priceless!

Old English
SCRATCH REMOVING POLISH
25¢

Old English Scratch Cover Polish, for "Furniture, Woodwork and Floors." *Davis Collection.* Polish $15-$18.

Promoted in April 1943, "Old English Scratch Removing Polish" sold for only 25¢ a bottle.

Self-polishing Aerowax floor wax. "will not yellow." *Davis Collection.* $20-$25.

Kresge Household Polish was made with "genuine cedar oil" and sold only at Kresge's. *Davis Collection.* $75-$100.

"New . . . Longer Lasting!" Aerowax in one pint metal container could be used for all floors. *Davis Collection.* $15-$20.

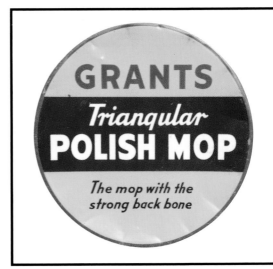

Have Lovelier Floors...with LESS CARE!

Give Floors the Same Longer Lasting Beauty that Makes SIMONIZ so Famous for Cars

You'll be amazed how much more beautiful the now famous Self-Polishing SIMONIZ makes your floors. Spread with cloth or mop applicator... no rubbing, no buffing... it shines as it dries crystal-clear on floors. A damp cloth keeps them sparkling... removes dust, dirt, soiled spots, spilled things. Get Self-Polishing SIMONIZ today!

THE SIMONIZ COMPANY, CHICAGO 16, ILLINOIS

Sold by grocery, hardware, variety, drug, paint, 5 cents to $1, auto accessory and department stores—and by linoleum dealers everywhere

Self-Polishing SIMONIZ FOR FLOORS
Shines as it Dries

Self-Polishing SIMONIZ FOR FLOORS

"Self-Polishing" Simoniz for floors was advertised in 1946.

Grants Triangular Polish Mop No. 607. "The Mop with the strong back bone." The special, patented construction of this mop made it much stronger and more durable than any other type of mop. It could be used for "cleaning, dusting and polishing all varnished or painted floors, and linoleum." Manufactured For W.T. Grant Company. $45-$50.

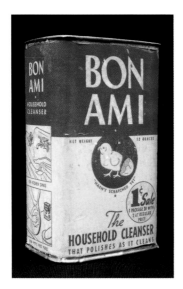

"Bon Ami" household cleanser. *Davis Collection.* $15-$18.

Johnson's BLEM in original carton with disposable application pads. *Davis Collection.* $15-$20.

Advertised as "The NEW Plasticolor Clothespins" in January, 1947, these moderately priced clothespins sold 12 for 25¢ or 49 for $1.00. Manufactured by Mastro Plastics Corp. New York, N.Y. *Davis Collection.* $2-$3 each.

"LITTLE JIM" No. 115

- Attractive colors—yellow, red, white, aquamarine, coral
- Finest quality miniature light ever made
- Small, compact... practical, powerful
- Optically perfect, aluminized reflector

ACTUAL SIZE

69¢ Without Battery

No. 115 "Little Jim" Pocket Lite uses 1 "Eveready" No. 915 Battery and "Eveready" Lamp No. 112

No. 15 Display Package
features 12 No. 115 "Little Jim" lights

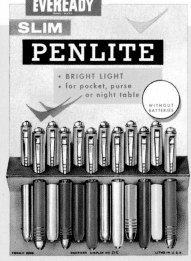

No. 21C Display Package features 12 No. 212 Slim Penlites. Available individually boxed, in all-chrome.

SLIM PENLITE No. 212

- Eye-catching colors—yellow, pink, blue, red, green, grey, white, all-chrome
- Ideal for Doctors, Nurses
- For Pocket, Purse or Night Table
- Bright Light... Long Life

89¢ Without Batteries

No. 212 Penlite uses 2 "Eveready" No. 912 Batteries and "Eveready" Lamp No. 224

SEE OTHER SIDE FOR COMPLETE PRICE INFORMATION

ACTUAL SIZE

The famous and fast-selling Eveready™ Pocket Lites, promoted during the 1950s as "New Decorator Colors and Popular Priced."

103

new  EVEREADY
HEAVY-DUTY QUALITY *penlite*

ACTUAL SIZE

List Price
98¢
without batteries

ENGINEERED FOR | **PROFESSIONAL INDUSTRIAL OTHER PRACTICAL USES**

- Lamp hoods in attractive decorator colors — red, turquoise, white. Provide brighter beam — more light.
- Positive, plunger-type 3-way switch — "off"..."on"..."flasher".

No. 230 Penlite
Uses 2 "Eveready"
No. 915 Batteries
and "Eveready"
Lamp No. 222.

No. 23 Display Package features 12 No. 230 Penlites with colored hoods. Available individually boxed with white hood.

SUGGESTED DEALER ORDER

	DEALER	LIST
1 "Eveready" No. 23 Display Package (12 No. 230 Penlites at $0.65 each) . .	$ 7.80	$11.76
24 "Eveready" No. 915 Flashlight Batteries @ $.095 each . .	2.28	3.60
TOTAL SUGGESTED DEALER COST	$10.08	—
TOTAL LIST VALUE	—	$15.36
DEALER PROFIT	$ 5.28	(34.4%)

"Eveready", "Nine Lives" with the Cat Symbol and "Union Carbide" are registered trade-marks of Union Carbide Corporation

NATIONAL CARBON COMPANY
Division of Union Carbide Corporation
30 East 42nd Street, New York 17, N. Y.
Sales Offices: Atlanta, Chicago, Dallas, Kansas City, Los Angeles, New York, Pittsburgh, San Francisco
IN CANADA: Union Carbide Canada Limited, Toronto

Original 1952 advertisement for the new Eveready "Heavy-Duty Quality Penlite," shown with store display package.

Below and next two pages:
Original 1959 advertisements for a selection of Eveready Shop Lites, Masterlite Flashlights, American Lites, and Special Purpose Lites. Flashlights and related merchandise have recently become highly collectible. Values for these and the selection of other flashlights that follows have not been provided due to significant geographical differences.

EVEREADY
TRADE-MARK

"MASTERLITE" FLASHLIGHTS

- Square for easy grip . . . smart styling
- Heavy-gauge chrome-plated seamless metal case
- Optically perfect aluminized reflector
- Lamp shock absorber
- Unbreakable polyethylene lens-guard . . . prevents rolling
- 3-way deluxe lock switch . . . "off," "on" and "flasher"

**7251 DELUXE STANDARD
2-CELL IN ALL-METAL**

In Display Package 72. Uses 2 No. 950 or D99 and Lamp No. PR2.

72 DISPLAY PACKAGE

Contains 6 No. 7251 All-Metal "Masterlite" Flashlights.

	Per Package	Per Light
List Price	$11.70	$1.95
Suggested Dealer Price	7.80	1.30

**7251P DELUXE STANDARD
2-CELL WITH LENS GUARD**

In Display Package 72P6 or individually boxed. Uses 2 No. 950 or D99 and Lamp No. PR2.

72P6 DISPLAY PACKAGE

Features 6 No. 7251P "Masterlite" Flashlights.

	Per Package	Per Light
List Price	$11.70	$1.95
Suggested Dealer Price	7.80	1.30

7231P BABY 2-CELL

In Display Package 31 or individually boxed. Uses 2 No. 935 and Lamp No. PR4.

31 DISPLAY PACKAGE

Features 6 No. 7231P Baby "Masterlite" Flashlights.

	Per Package	Per Light
List Price	$11.10	$1.85
Suggested Dealer Price	7.38	1.23

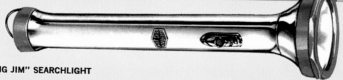

7552P 5-CELL "BIG JIM" SEARCHLIGHT

Powerful, long-range beam. Large non-rolling head. Removable bottom cap. Ring hanger. Individually boxed. Uses 5 No. 950 or D99 and Lamp No. PR12.

List Price, Each $4.95
Suggested Dealer Price 3.31

7352P 3-CELL "BIG JIM" SEARCHLIGHT

Large non-rolling head. Powerful beam. Removable bottom cap. Ring hanger. Individually boxed. Uses 3 No. 950 or D99 and Lamp No. PR3.

List Price, Each $3.95
Suggested Dealer Price 2.64

EVEREADY _ALL AMERICAN_ LITES
TRADE-MARK

- Budget-priced in eye-catching decorator colors
- Heavy-gauge, chrome-plated seamless metal case
- Durable, color-matched jumbo switch
- Optically perfect aluminized reflector
- Unbreakable polyethylene lens-guard

319 STANDARD 2-CELL
In Display Packages 130-B or 130-BC. Uses 2 No. 950 or D99 and Lamp No. PR2.

*130A All American Display (7 3251 Flashlights) available at present pricing indefinitely.

130-B DISPLAY PACKAGE *
Contains 14 No. 319 Standard 2-Cell All Americans — 4 red, 4 black, 2 white, 2 turquoise, 2 coral. 2 LIGHTS FREE with PURCHASE of 12!

	Per Package	Per Light
List Price	$16.66	$1.19
Suggested Dealer Price	9.84	0.82

130-BC DISPLAY PACKAGE
Same as 130-B except comes with individual display sleeves.

---

339 BABY 2-CELL
In Display Package 39. Uses 2 No. 935 and Lamp No. PR4.

39 DISPLAY PACKAGE
Features 6 No. 339 Baby 2-Cell All Americans—2 white, 2 black, 2 red.

	Per Package	Per Light
List Price	$5.94	$0.99
Suggested Dealer Price	4.08	0.68

329 STANDARD 3-CELL
In Display Package 29 or individually boxed (red). Uses 3 No. 950 and Lamp No. PR3.

29 DISPLAY PACKAGE
Contains 6 No. 329 Standard 3-Cell — 2 red, 2 white, 2 black — with individual display sleeves.

	Per Package	Per Light
List Price	$10.14	$1.69
Suggested Dealer Price	6.78	1.13

SPECIAL PURPOSE LITES

2T5 and 2T3 TORCH LITES
Come with 5" or 3" signal wand, visible up to ½ mile (2T5 shown). Piercing white beam. Jumbo switch. Both types available in Display Package 35 or individually boxed. Use 2 No. 950 or D99 and Lamp No. PR2.

35 DISPLAY PACKAGE
Features 3 No. 2T5 and 3 No. 2T3 Torch Lites.

	Per Package	Per Light 2T3	2T5
List Price	$8.04	$1.39	$1.49
Suggested Dealer Price	5.28	0.91	0.97

3452 HEAD-LITE
Gives bright light...leaves both hands free. Broad, comfortable head band. Long-range beam. Waterproof-rustproof features. For fishermen, sportsmen, mechanics, etc. Uses 510S 6-volt battery and Lamp No. PR13.

List Price, Each $2.75
Suggested Dealer Price 1.83

1348 BATTERY CARRYING POUCH
(For Use With 3452 Head-Lite)
Rugged. Rainproof. Fits easily on belt or strap. Specially designed to take "Eveready" No. 510S 6-volt Battery.

List Price, Each $0.69
Suggested Dealer Price 0.46

318 COMPASS LITE

Powerful flashlight with accurate, shock-resistant compass in head...easily readable day or night. Jumbo switch. In Display Package 18 or individually boxed. Uses 2 No. 950 or D99 and Lamp No. PR2.

18 DISPLAY PACKAGE
Features 6 No. 318 Compass Lites.

	Per Package	Per Light	Ind. Boxed
List Price	$9.54	$1.59	$1.69
Suggested Dealer Price	6.30	1.05	1.12

The Stationery Department

School supplies, stationery, and arts and craft materials could be purchased at any local five-and-ten-cent store. These reasonably priced items could be found in a separate department without much assistance.

In 1929, F.W. Woolworth listed provisions "For School" as composition books, pencil tablets, pen tablets, looseleaf books and fillers, memorandum books and pads, lead pencils and sharpeners, mechanical pencils and extra lead, crayons, pencil cabinets, penholder and points, crepe papers, erasers, Waterman's ink, white paste, and mucilage.

Customers of the five-and-ten could also find an assortment of everyday stationery, both looseleaf and gift sets that included envelopes. A variety of greeting cards and wrapping paper was also available.

War times were letter writing times, resulting in a stupendous use of stationery. During World War II, people in business, in the home, and those in the armed forces stepped up the demand to an all time peak. The variety stores made an effort to expand their sales of this important line.

This selection of "Onward Inks, Pastes and Mucilage" was issued on April 7, 1942. No. 2510B, Free-Flo washable blue, Onward 1-1/2 oz. cube bottle, metal screw cap lacquered to match color of ink. No. 2519B, DeLuxe blue black, 3 oz. cube bottle, metallic Onward label, cap enameled to match color of ink. No. 2706B, Onward 2 oz. jar of white potato dextrine paste with wood spreader, blue cap. No. 2700B, Onward 3 oz. tube of white potato dextrine paste. No. 2726B, Onward 4 oz. jar of white potato dextrine paste with wood spreader, red cap. No. 2702B, Onward 1-1/2 oz. square bottle dextrine mucilage with wood spreader, red cap. No. 2801B, Onward 1 oz. dextrine mucilage in a new shaped bottle with red rubber spreader tip. No. 2729, Crescent 3/4" x 5" lead tube airplane cement. $8-$12 each.

TESTORS ... PASTE AND MUCILAGE

This Nationally Advertised brand of paste, mucilage and cements need no introduction! Their strong adhesive, fast drying qualities, make them a fast-moving everyday seller. Now, more than ever before Mr. and Mrs. "Customer" are "mending-it." Mending is no longer a patriotic gesture . . . but is rapidly becoming a growing necessity The "tiniest" of broken pieces can be held securely in place by applying a small quantity of these well known adhesives. Order a sufficient supply to meet the demand of household, school and office. Order now!

WHITE PASTE	WHITE PASTE	JUMBO SIZE TUBE
5c. 1¾ oz. liquid oz. jar, red dome shape closure. Exceptionally creamy and smooth, with pleasant odor. Wood spreader.	10c. ¼ pint jar. Red dome shape closure, pleasant odor, wood spreader with each jar. Soft creamy texture.	5c. 2-liquid oz. Pure white paste, exceptionally smooth, dries hard and fast. Beautifully lithographed 3-color tube.
86X-15—(86R2708) 3 doz in ctn., 10 lbs . . . . Doz **.38**	**86X-15Q**—1 doz in ctn., 7 lbs . . . . Doz **.67**	**86X-15A**—3 doz in ctn., 8½ lbs . . . . Doz **.36**

MUCILAGE	MUCILAGE—FEEDER TOP	MUCILAGE
5c. 1¾. liquid Oz. jar. quick drying heavy and smooth. Wood spreader with each jar.	10c. 2½ Oz. Extra Large, Modernistic shaped bottle with spreader top, glue feeds from bottle mouth, *no fuss or muss!*	10c. ¼ pint jar. Pure dextrin adhesive for all paper. Wood spreader with each jar. Smooth heavy adhesive.
86X-16A—3 doz in ctn., 10 lbs . . . . Doz **.38**	**86X-16B**—(86-2815)—1 doz in ctn., 5 lbs . . . . Doz **.67**	**86X-16Q**—1 doz in ctn., 8 lbs . . . . Doz **.67**

TERMS—Net 30 days from 10th of following month.
SHIPPED—F.O.B.—Rockford, Ill.
MINIMUM SHIPMENT—$10.00.

TIME OF SHIPMENT—About 10 days after factory receives order.

PRICES—Subject to change or withdrawal without notice.

In 1943, "Testors" needed no introduction. This nationally advertised brand of paste, mucilage, and cement was known for its strong adhesive and fast drying qualities, which made these products fast-moving sellers. A sufficient supply was kept to meet the demand from households, schools, and offices. This original "TESTORS . . . Paste and Mucilage" advertisement was issued April 6, 1943 $8-$12 each.

GLUE, MODEL AIRPLANE CEMENT
and HOUSEHOLD CEMENT...

The adhesive that meets all needs! Mends glass, wood, metal, and china ... quick drying ... sure to stick. The model Airplane cement is the "Big Item" in model airplane building, its quick drying, fast-sticking speeds the airplane production! They are an all year round need and fast sellers! Plan now to order a sufficient supply.

2 OZ. TUBE

10c.— 3-color metal tube with screw eye closure. Ideal as adhesive for wood. Strong, lightweight, dries quickly. Waterproof, has a pleasant wintergreen odor. It sticks and stays stuck!

86X-7A—1 doz in ctn., 31 lbs.. Doz **.62**

1¼ OZ. JAR

10c. 1¼ liquid ounce. Attractive glass container with screw cap. Pleasant odor. A wood spreader with each con'ainer. Quick drying, sure stick. A necessary item around the household.

86X-7—(86-2926) 1 doz in ctn. 3½ lbs.............................. Doz **.60**

AIRPLANE CEMENT

HOUSEHOLD CEMENT

HOUSEHOLD CEMENT

10c. ¾ x 4 in. Tube —s c r e w-eye closure. Sodium silicate, water white in color. Especially recommended for adhesive of *china and glass*. Will stand boiling water. Transparent, dries quickly. The screw-eye top with its pin dot opening, releases just the required amount.

86X-3—1 doz in ctn., 1½ lbs ....Doz **.62**

Crystal Clear Cement

10c. ¾ x 4 in. Tube, screw eye top with pin dot opening releasing just the required amount. A clear crystal pyroxylin cement. Mends articles such as crockery, wood, leather etc. Waterproof, flexible, dries quickly, holds tenaciously.

86X-2—(86-2929). 1 ctn., 1½ lbs....Doz **.67**

AIRPLANE CEMENT

A cement for all kinds of airplane model building. It's waterproof, quick drying, very strong and light in weight. Its crystal clearness makes plane modeling look smooth as glass. The two size tubes 5 and 10c size are very popular. Now more than ever before both young and old are building model planes. Airplane cement affords quicker assembly and a sure "stick-together." The worst forced landing cannot tear the cemented pieces apart. Be sure to have a sufficient supply of both sizes.

86X-50A—(62-7900) 3 doz. in ctn., 2½ lbs.
Retail at 5c .... Doz **.37**
86X-5A—(62-7906) 1 doz. in ctn., 1½ lbs.
Retail at 10c .... Doz **.65**

WARNING—Retail prices suggested herein must not be used unless they are no higher than YOUR ceiling as established under the General Maximum Price Regulation, or any other applicable regulation.

Original advertisement for Testors glue, model airplane cement, and household cement, products that met all the requirements for mending glass, wood, metal, and china. The model airplane cement was the "Big Item" in model airplane building. These adhesives were quick drying and available year round. $8-$12 each.

WE HOPE THAT YOU ENJOY THIS BOOK...and that it will occupy a proud place in your library. We would like to keep you informed about other publications from Schiffer Books. Please return this card with your requests and comments.

Title of Book Purchased _____   ☐ hard cover ☐ soft cover

☐ Purchased at: _____   ☐ received as a gift

Comments or ideas for books you would like to see us publish: _____

_____

Your Name: _____

Address _____

City _____ State ____ Zip____ E-mail Address _____

☐ Please send me a **free** Schiffer Antiques, Collectibles, Arts and Design Catalog
☐ Please send me a **free** Schiffer Woodcarving, Woodworking, and Crafts Catalog
☐ Please send me a **free** Schiffer Military, Aviation, and Automotive History Catalog
☐ Please send me a **free** Whitford Body, Mind, and Spirit Catalog
☐ Please send me information about new releases via email.

See our most current books on the web at **www.schifferbooks.com**

Contact us at: Phone: 610-593-1777; Fax: 610-593-2002; or E-mail: schifferbk@aol.com
SCHIFFER BOOKS ARE CURRENTLY AVAILABLE FROM YOUR BOOKSELLER

K: user.do\wp\basic\bounceback

SCHIFFER PUBLISHING LTD
4880 LOWER VALLEY ROAD
ATGLEN, PA 19310-9717

CARTER'S INK PRODUCTS

(See your listing for full information.)

CUBES

No. 816

No. 866

No. 886

No. 966

No. 526

No. 46

No. 56

No. 176

SPECIALTIES

No. 10HP

No. 359

No. 990

No. 998

No. 442

No. C439

No. 412

No. C438

No. 409

No. C484

5¢ WINNER INKS 5¢

No. 919

No. 989

No. 969

No. 979

(See over for other important items)

This original "Carter's Ink Products, Cubes and Specialties" advertisement dates to the 1940s. No. 816-No. 176, $5-$10 each. No. 10HP, $20-$25 complete. No. 359-No. 979, $10-$15 each.

CARTER'S INK PRODUCTS

See your listing for full information.

ADHESIVES

No. 727

No. 157

No. 343

No. 367

No. 255

No. 233

No. 629

No. C 469

No. C499

No. C289

No. C465

No. C239

5¢ WINNER ADHESIVES 5¢

No. 937

No. 939
(See over for other important items)

No. 929

No. 925

Another Carter's advertisement from the 1940s, this one for "Carter's Ink Products, Adhesives and Winner Adhesives." No. 727-No. 367, $15-$20 each. No. 255-No. 925, $8-$12 each.

"Woolco" red stamp pad. *Davis Collection.* $5-$8.

This "Carter's School Paste" jar recently sold for $25.00. The colorful illustration on the paper label and the condition of the jar were the selling factors for this product. If the label had been removed, no indication of the contents would be known and the jar would be worthless. *Davis Collection.* $45-$55.

F.W. Woolworth pads of forty sheets each, "Pocket Secretary Refill and Memo Pad" and "Loose Leaf Address Book Refill." Both marked "Dist. By. F.W. Woolworth Co., New York, N.Y. 10007." *Davis Collection.* $5-$8 each complete.

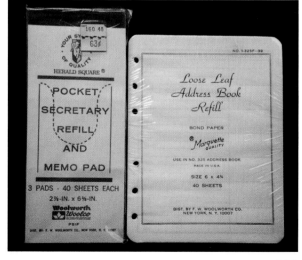

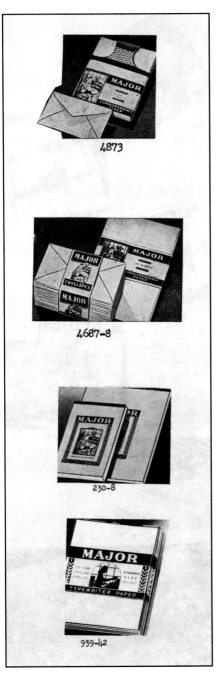

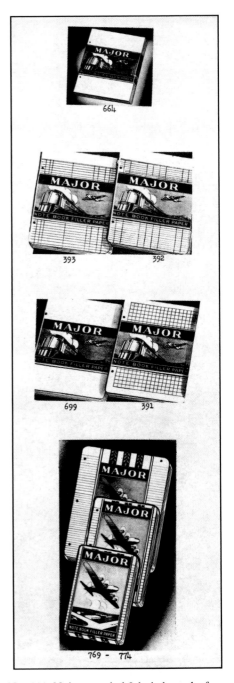

"Major" packaged paper and envelopes, issued August 25, 1942. No. 4873, eighteen double sheets and envelopes in printed jacket-white vellum finish. No. 4687-8, thirty flat sheets banded white vellum finish paper, unruled. No. 230-8, Major writing tables in 5" x 8" note size or 8" x 10" letter size. No. 939-42, Major typewriter paper. $10-$15 each complete.

No. 664, Major unruled 2-hole loose leaf fillers. No. 393 and 392, 10-1/2" x 8" double entry ledger ruled and journal ruled. No. 699 and 391, drawing paper and Science ruled. No. 769-774, Major narrow ruled with no marginal line, with marginal line, and regular ruled with marginal line. $10-$15 complete.

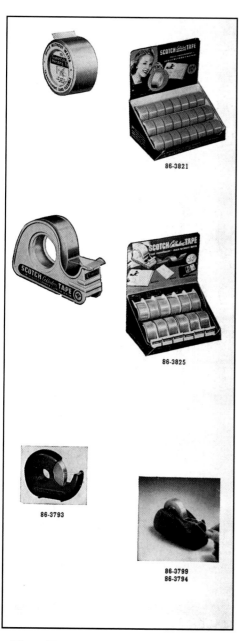

These "Scotch Cellulose Tape" products were issued April 7, 1942. No. 86-3821, cabinet display of Scotch Transparent included 3/4" rolls of tape for mending torn pages and documents. No. 86-3825, cabinet display of Scotch Transparent included 3" ivory color enameled metal dispensers. No. 86-3793, plastic hand or householder dispenser. No. 86-3799 (Mahogany) and 86-3794 (Ivory), desk dispensers held 1/2" and 3/4" tape. Cabinet Display $30-$40 each complete. Dispensers $8-$12 each.

An original 1945 "Scotch Cellulose Tape" advertisement, noting the wartime uses for this well-known tape.

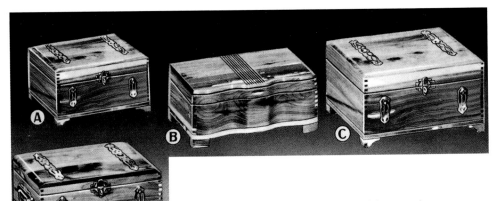

This selection of stationery chests without stationery was issued in a promotional advertisement to variety stores June 2, 1942. (A) 8-3/8" long polished red cedar with brass trimmings on top, front and hasp on front. (B) 10" long curved front polished beaded panel cover, paneled edge, and footed bottom. (C) genuine aromatic cedar complete with padlock and key, brass trimmings on top and front. (D) streamlined chest with footed bottom, brass handles, hasp, lock and key, hinges and trim. (E) red cedar chest with curved front, beveled top, beveled extension bottom, brass handles and hasp. $80-$90 each complete.

These stationery products were issued June 2, 1942. No. 4089, assorted juvenile die-cut boxed stationery. No. 4291, folded note sheets. No. 6152, assorted Christmas folded stationery. No. 4214, utility tray boxes. No. 4216, Holland patriotic addressed envelopes. No. 4419, Holland white linen paper in printed box. No. 4203, white vellum finish paper with paper covered Hunting scene box. $8-$12 each complete.

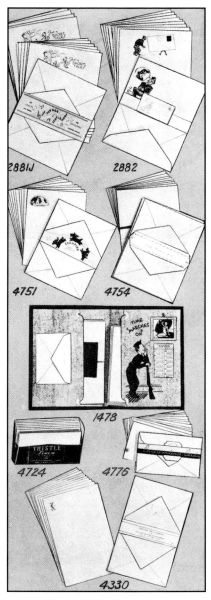

Customers could select one of thirty-four colors from the poster paper sample chart shown above. This poster paper could be cut or folded for use in designing posters, costumes, and interior decoration. A number and the color is indicated on each sample. ©1931 The Dobson-Evans Co., Columbus, Ohio, and Detroit, Michigan. Backstamped "G.C. Murphy Co." *Davis Collection.* Sample Chart $35-$40 complete.

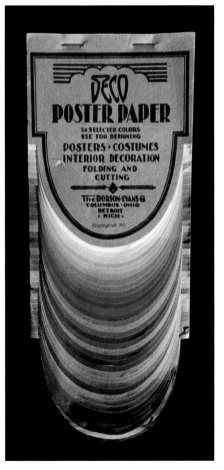

Packaged stationery issued June 2, 1942. No. 2881J, Jitterbug with four assorted designs. No. 2882, Right face with two assorted designs. No. 4751, Champion doggie stationery with four designs. No. 4754, dainty bordered personal stationery. No. 1478, correspondence portfolio. No. 4724, Thistle linen gilt edge correspondence cards and envelopes. No. 4776, gilt edge correspondence cards and envelopes. No. 4330, tinted border personal stationery. No. 1478, $10-$15 complete. Nos. 2881J, 2882, 4751, 4754, 4724, 4776, 4330, $8-$12 each complete.

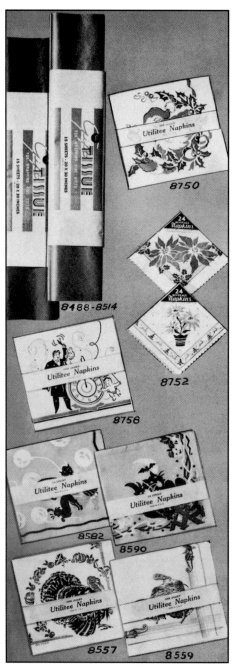

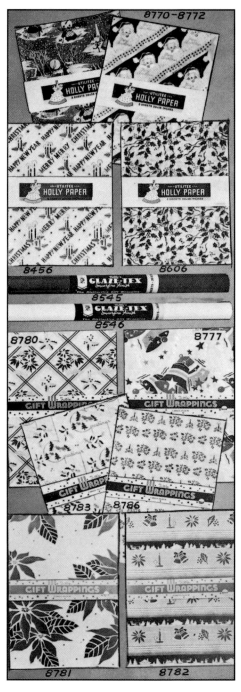

This assortment of paper supplies was promoted May 11, 1943. No. 8488-8514, tissue paper in assorted colors. No. 8750, embossed napkins. No. 8752, cocktail napkins. No. 8758, assorted New Years design napkins. No. 8582-8590, Halloween embossed napkins. No. 8557-8559, Thanksgiving embossed napkins. $15-$20 each complete pkg.

Wrapping paper assortment. No. 8770-8772, 8456-8606, Yuletide wrapping paper. No. 8545-8546, Glaze-Tex, a heavy weight glass finish on spiral wound core. No. 8780, 8777, 8783, 8786, water color gift wrapping paper on white background. No. 8781, 8782, water color gift wrapping paper on solid color background. $10-$15 complete pkg.

Sewing and Needlework

When World War I made it impossible to import the well-known D.M.C. cotton of which Woolworth's had been selling large quantities, Woolworth's approached an American spinner to make a similar product exclusively for them that would be equal in quality to D.M.C. This was the beginning of the famous "Woolco" crochet cotton, which since 1914 has become the most popular. The first order in 1914 was for 3,500 boxes and in 1918 was increased by many thousands.

In 1916, the following appeared in the *Woolco Knitting & Crocheting Manual*:

> In preparing the Woolco Manual, it has been our aim to produce a book that will be of greatest service both to those who are taking up the work for the first time and for those who need only new ideas for practical and pretty garments. All explanations have been selected for their general usefulness and good style.
>
> To those who are not familiar with knitting and crocheting with yarns a word of advice about yarn quality is important. In any line of goods quality is always worth its price, and in the end will prove the most economical. But while in some lines of goods a little better or a little worse may make slight difference, in yarns it means the difference between success and failure. The best worker in the world cannot make a satisfactory garment of inferior yarns. For this reason we wish to impress upon you the necessity of buying Woolco Yarns. You will then be certain to secure the full value of the time and skill you spend upon your work.
>
> The rapidity with which Woolco Yarns have established themselves among our patrons is the best possible testimony to their splendid qualities. Each of the three yarns are made from wools carefully selected to give the proper strength and character, every step in the long process of manufacture is closely watched and the finished yarn undergoes a final searching examination before it is boxed. That is why you can count on Woolco Yarns being always the same.
>
> When worked up into garments you will find that Woolco Yarns give an unusually soft and warm fabric with remarkable wearing qualities. Since a large part of the value of any knitted or crocheted garment is in the time and skill spent in making it, you should take particular care in the selection of your yarn. If you make it a point to use only Woolco Yarns, you can depend upon the finished garment giving perfect satisfaction.

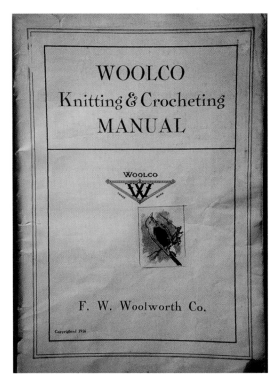

This 80-page softcover *Woolco Knitting & Crocheting Manual* provided instructions for making afghans, baby and children's wear, gloves, and sweaters. ©1916 F.W. Woolworth Co. *Schneider Collection.* $50-$60.

The back page of the *Woolco Knitting & Crocheting Manual* provided a listing of the latest crochet books. They were priced at 10¢ each and sold at F.W. Woolworth's Co.'s stores. Customers who could not obtain any of the books at their local store could remit the price plus 4¢ to F.W. Woolworth Co., 490 Washington St., Boston, Mass. *Schneider Collection.* $50-$60.

120

Woolworth customers were also advised that the "well-known condition of the dyestuffs market at present forces us to buy dyes in small lots so that we are no longer able to maintain our usual uniformity of shades. . . Buy enough yarn to finish your garment and see that it matches before you leave the store. By doing so you will avoid disappointment for yourself and assist us in overcoming an awkward and regrettable situation."

Woolworth's also provided a list of their materials. Woolco Knitting Worsted came sixteen skeins to a box and was priced at 10¢ for the skein. This was an unusually strong yarn, made especially for use in garments subject to hard wear. Knitting Worsted was a favorite for sweaters, stockings, and all kinds of outer garments. Colors available were: black, white, cardinal, garnet, blue, navy, khaki, brown mixed, gray mixed, dark gray mixed, and blue mixed.

Woolco Germantown Zephyr was the most useful of yarns. It was a full, smooth thread and gave satisfactory service in all classes of garments. Colors available were: cream white, snow white, black, cardinal 1, cardinal 2 (darker), garnet, wood brown, seal, lavender, purple, pink, rose pink, light blue, medium blue, navy, yellow, old rose, silver gray, steel, yellow green, and oxford. It also sold at 10¢ for the skein.

Woolco Shetland Floss was a light, fluffy yarn made for lightweight garments—shawls, kimonos, lightweight sweaters, baby-wear, and scarfs. Colors available were: cream white, snow white, black, pink, blue, navy, lilac, heliotrope, steel, cardinal, and garnet. Shetland Floss was priced at 10¢ the skein; 2¢ postage was added per skein.

In addition to yarns, the five-and-ten-cent-stores offered a variety of other sewing needs. In 1929, Woolworth published a list of such items that included: art pillow tops and backs, six strand embroidery cotton, rayon rope embroidery in skeins, embroidery hoops and flat pieces for embroidering, dresser scarfs, centerpieces, boudoir pillow tops and backs, tape measures, sewing cottons, needles of all sizes, colored mercerized threads, darning cottons and snap fasteners, art fringes, imported French laces, Val laces, Torchon, cluny, Venice and art laces for trimming curtains, pillow cases and bed spreads, ribbons for trimming, thimbles, scissors, super fine tapes, lawn bias bindings, pins, safety pins, pearl buttons, and the latest in patterns.

Also sold at most F.W. Woolworth Co. stores were the latest and most popular crochet books and cross stitch designs. Each publication sold for 10¢ each and could be purchased directly from the F.W. Woolworth Co., 490 Washington St., Boston, Massachusetts if unavailable at any store.

Woolco snap fasteners were found in the notions section of the F.W. Woolworth stores. These fasteners appeared in the publication *Woolworth's First 75 Years 1879-1954,* ©1954. $5-$8 complete.

The Woolworth Needle Book had seventy-nine assorted needles and sold for 15¢. *Davis Collection.* $15-$20.

ENJOY SMOOTH SEWING—
more quality for your money with
MILWARDS
NEEDLES 10¢
QUALITY FOR OVER 200 YEARS

SHARPS 3/9

MILWARDS NEEDLES
MADE IN ENGLAND
LARGE EYE NEEDLES

HERE'S WHY:

1. Thread doesn't fray and break...eyes are smooth inside. Seams are stronger because thread isn't weakened by rough eyes.

2. Needles slip through material with ease because points are hardened to stay sharp, gradually tapered, and polished to gem-smoothness.

3. Better work—no bulging eyes to make big holes in fabric.

4. Needles won't bend out of shape or snap in ordinary use ... because Milwards are made of expertly tempered English Sheffield steel.

Get Milwards at notions counters.

A MEMBER OF THE FAMOUS COATS & CLARK'S O.N.T. THREAD FAMILY

The advantages of Milwards needles, which could be purchased at notions counters, were described in this advertisement. Circa 1955.

This selection of seam binding and bias tape has the original Murphy's price tag. *Davis Collection*. $5-$8 each.

Yard sticks were available in the sewing department of most five-and ten-cent stores. Those shown here read "Shop Woolworth's First For Better Values," W.T. Grant Company "Known For Values Since 1906," "McCrory's 5-10-25¢ Store Gives You Self-Service Shopping," "Shop At McCrory's And Save," and "Compliments of TG&Y Serving Communities In 30 States Coast To Coast." *Davis Collection*. $18-$20 each.

S.S. Kresge Stores offered various needlework catalogs. These catalogs are dated 1936, 1938, 1940, and 1943. *Davis Collection.* $15-$20 each.

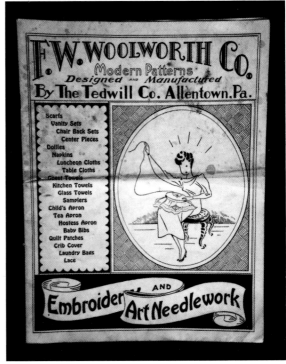

F.W. Woolworth Co. *Modern Patterns Designed and Manufactured by The Tedwill Co. Allentown, Pa.* This 8-1/2" x 11" publication provided instructions for making an assortment of embroidery and artwork. *Private Collection.* $20-$25.

These Vogart needlecraft novelties were "Made Exclusively for S.S. Kresge Co." This 7" x 8-3/4" publication from Spring and Summer, 1935 provided instructions for making an assortment of boudoir scarfs, tea aprons, decorative pot-holder sets, centerpieces, pictures, and novelty pillows. *Davis Collection.* $20-$25.

Vogue Art Needlework Novelties, Fall Catalog 1935. Original designs by Vogart, this time made exclusively for Woolworth's. *Davis Collection.* $20-$25.

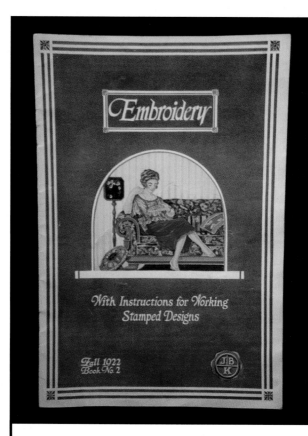

All material with stamped designs illustrated in this 7"
x 10" *Embroidery* publication from 1922 were sold in
F.W. Woolworth Co. stores. *Private Collection*. $40-$50.

GIFTS YOU CAN MAKE
by Ann Bucilla

NEEDLEWORK IDEAS...EASY TO DO...ECONOMICAL TOO

What's Christmas without toys for little folks to cuddle? Bucking Bronco here is just one of many cute (and *safe*) snuggle pets you can make so quickly with **BUCILLA** stamped toy designs. Others? The Three Little Bears ...Hansel and Gretel ... Bess the Cow and her frolicsome calf. So much fun to embroider with gay-colored **BUCILLA** thread, you'll want to make them all!

No frosty fingers in your family this winter, if you tend to your **Bear Brand** knitting now! For easy-to-make gifts, get this Gloves and Mittens Book (Vol. 19). Rugged sport gloves for the menfolks ... peasant mittens for the children ... smart town styles for sisters and cousins and aunts. Only 15¢ for 23 clever designs! At your pet needlework counter. Or write to me enclosing 15¢.

"Sleepy-time Pals" make delightful gifts ...brighten any nursery ...make it sport for small fry to go to bed. A yawning bunny and a happy puppy are the theme of this **BUCILLA** ensemble ... so easy to embroider and applique! The set includes 2 bound bibs, a crib cover, a pillow, 2 terry towels, 2 pictures *and* 2 huggable toys. Buy the whole set or any part of it. At your favorite needlework store.

Bucilla
for 77 years the first name in
NEEDLEWORK
230 Fifth Avenue, New York I, N. Y.

Doilie-Craft by F.W. Woolworth Co. was available in the notions counter and came with complete instructions. *Davis Collection.* $25-$30 complete.

The "Bear Brand Yarns" promoted in this 1944 advertisement were made by Bucilla.

How to skirt a home-sewing hazard!

The "wrong" slide fastener can cause plenty of trouble!
So take a tip from the professionals! Choose a *special*
Talon slide fastener for each individual closing need!
That's the way to help insure slick, smooth fit...and
dependable service!

IT'S THE BLUE PACKAGE
for the supple Talon placket
fastener. It's a cinch to sew
in...won't creep down or
stick at the top, thanks to the
patented bridge top-stop.

IT'S THE ROSE PACKAGE
for the sturdy Talon skirt
fastener. Specially designed
to withstand waistline strain
...with the exclusive auto-
matic self-lock to prevent
accidental opening.

IT'S THE ORANGE PACKAGE
for the slim, dainty Talon
neckline fastener. Easy-to-follow
directions in every package.

"TALON"

Reg. U.S. Pat. Off. Talon, Inc., Meadville, Pa.

The Dependable Slide Fastener

TALON

9 INCH
NAVY

for DRESS PLACKETS
ONLY

BRIDGE TOP-STOP

"THIN AS A SEAM"

"Easy
to sew
in"

TALON

Because of military
demands, you may
have difficulty at times
in finding the par-
ticular Talon fastener
you need. But keep
trying! It's worth it!

A T   N O T I O N   C O U N T E R S   E V E R Y W H E R E

Talon was the "dependable
slide fastener" and
available at notion counters
everywhere. This original
advertisement is dated
1945.

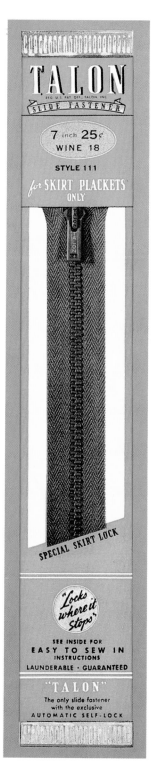

This aluminum finished display cabinet was free to stores with an order of six dozen Talon fasteners. It required only 13" of counter space.

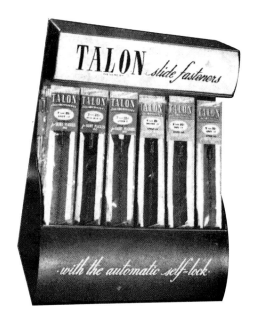

Talon slide fastener package "for skirt plackets only," Style 111 in Wine.

Six dozen of the best-selling slide fastener colors could be displayed in this lighted Talon case. It measures 12-1/4" long, 7-3/4" wide, and 15" high. $30-$40 complete.

This free, six-page *Simplicity Fashion Forecast* from September, 1937 was "Compliments of . . . S.S. Kresge Company." Included inside were complete illustrated and diagrammed sewing instructions for each Simplicity pattern available, plus various products sold at Kresge. *Davis Collection.* $15-$20 complete.

Right:
Short-Cuts to Sewing Success was fully illustrated with seventy-six pages, sold for 15¢, and was "Prepared By Du Barry Patterns for The F.W. Woolworth Co." *Davis Collection.* $30-$35 complete.

Du Barry Patterns for 10¢ and 15¢ from F.W. Woolworth Co. Date unknown. *Davis Collection.* $10-$18.

SOFT DRESSMAKER DETAIL

2480 B

5043

5036

5047

A tapering panel points up the soft bodice detail in this flattering afternoon frock. Size 36: 3¾ yards 39". Sizes 32, 34, 36, 38, 40, 42. Du Barry **5047**
Price 15c

Youthfully styled with flaring eight-gore skirt and molded bodice. Size 16: 3⅜ yards of 39" fabric. Sizes 12, 14, 16, 18, 20. Du Barry **5043**
Price 15c

The princess front contrasts with the curved waistline on either side. Size 16: 2¾ of 39", ¼ of 35" lace. Sizes 12 to 20. Du Barry **2480B**
Price 10c

Youthful bolero ensemble. Size 15: 1 yard 54" for bolero, 3½ yards 39", ⅜ yard 39" contrast. Sizes 11, 12, 13, 14, 15, 16, 18. Du Barry **5036**
Price 15c

Du Barry Patterns — 10c and 15c — F. W. Woolworth Co.

131

Betsy Ross Summer Fashions from June-July, 1933 sold for 10¢ and 15¢ at G.C. Murphy Company. These patterns featured the latest in fashion at the lowest prices. Betsy Ross Pattern Co. 1933. *Davis Collection.* $30-$40.

Below:
Le Chic buttons were available "at your favorite counter." Circa 1951. *Davis Collection.* $3-$5.

Distributed by F.W. Woolworth Co., this Woolworth/
Woolco precut two yards of "Western Bandanna" printed
material sold for $3.94 and was "Fashion cut for your
home sewing needs." This material could not be used for
children's sleep wear. *Davis Collection.* $5-$10 complete
with tag.

All over the country, "Press-On" products were telling women to simplify their sewing and mending. This display rack and mending tape earned extra dollars for dime stores. It was made of heavy metal wire, 14" long by 6-1/4" wide and stood 4" high in front and 6-1/4" in back. A display rack with refillable merchandise units was used in the Ben Franklin stores and issued March 10, 1942.

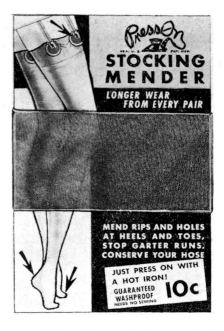

"Press-On" stocking mender. The required piece was cut to size and shape, then pressed into position with a hot iron. It was advertised to stop garter runs and reinforce the heels and toes of stockings. Available in tan color only. $6-$8 complete.

"Press-On" mending tape saved "Time, Energy, Money" and helped with many sewing tasks. It was guaranteed to withstand washing and dry cleaning. $6-$8 complete.

Pet Supplies

Pet supplies were often found at the rear of the store, along with goldfish and caged canaries. I am providing only those products that have been made available to me, as it would be impossible to provide a complete list of pet supplies that were available at the five-and-dime.

84X-606

84X-250

84X-241

No. 84X-606, two-sided phonograph record "Master Radio Canaries" with organ accompaniment. $15-$20 complete. No. 84X-250, cello wrapped seeded treat ball. $3-$5 complete. No. 84X-241, cello wrapped bird exerciser. $5-$8. No. 84X-408, skin ointment for ailments and bare spots. $8-$10. No. 84X-407, foot balm for treating sore feet. $8-$10.

84X-408

84X-407

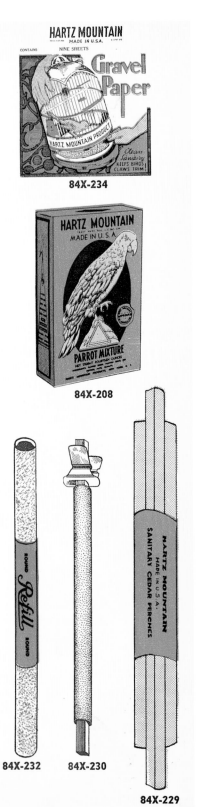

84X-234

84X-208

84X-232   84X-230

84X-229

No. 84X-234, gravel paper, six sheets per envelope. Three sizes, round, oblong and large. $3-$5 complete envelope. No. 84X-208, mixed 13 oz. Hartz Mountain parrot mixture. $15-$18 complete. No. 84X-232, sanded tube refills. $5-$8 complete. No. 84X-230, grip perches with sanded tube, cage clip and mite trap. $5-$8 complete. No. 84X-229, Hartz Mountain sanitary Cedar Perches. $5-$8 complete.

This **PLUS** in his diet

French's Bird Seed

Plus **Bird Biscuit**

puts **SONG** in his heart

STOP and think. You can't keep your canary happy on a humdrum diet— perhaps, not even healthy. He needs French's Bird Seed *and Biscuit*, which give him a *complete* and appetizing diet of 12 tested ingredients.

LOOK at him go for the *Biscuit!* There is one in every package of French's Bird Seed—chock-full of elements he would seek if he were out in nature. Feeding them in biscuit form is the *practical* way, and gives him extra exercise.

LISTEN for those glorious new notes after feeding this famous French's diet for ten days. More than likely, you'll be hearing trills you've never heard before!

French's
BIRD SEED and BISCUIT
THE LARGEST-SELLING BIRD DIET IN AMERICA

20

French's Bird Seed and Biscuit advertisement from October 1951. Bird Seed $15-$18.

French's Canary Bird Gravel, Kitty Chaperon 3 oz. powder,
Cenol Flea Powder, and Hartz Mountain Parakeet Treat in 3-1/2
oz. glass jar. *Davis Collection.* Treat $10-$12. Gravel $15-$18,
Chaperon $35-$40. Powder $15-$20.

Spaniel dog feeder in red by the McCoy Pottery
Company. *Dupler Collection.* $65-$75.

Garden Supplies

For the garden, dime stores carried flower and vegetable seeds—all kinds in season. Also found were Narcissus bulbs in season, lawn seeds in season (except in most southern stores of the U.S.) women's garden gloves, men's canvas work gloves, insect sprays, household wrapping twine, and trowels.

A free counter display card came with each carton of "2-Way" insecticide screen paint, which retailed at 49¢ a bottle. Issued April 21, 1942, this was a big profit-making opportunity for dime stores. It was available in 4 oz. and 8 oz. bottles with applicator. Insecticide $15-$20 complete. Display Card $35-$40 complete.

This advertisement for Kresge's seeds appeared in a May, 1940 issue of *Better Homes & Gardens.* "No Finer Seeds At Any Price!" Packaged Seeds $10-$15 per package.

"Tri-ogen" rose spray was a concentrated insect spray and fungicide for garden and greenhouse plants. Manufactured by The Rose Manufacturing Co., Beacon, N.Y. *Davis Collection.* $50-$60 complete.

Sold only at Kress stores, Dart Insect Spray was used to kill "flies, moths, roaches, mosquitoes, bed bugs, ants." 1/2 pint metal container. *Davis Collection.* $35-40.

The Federal "Mist-Maker Household Sprayer" could be used for spraying plants and, insecticides in the garden, as well as clothes, glass cleaner, moth proofing, liquids and deodorants inside. Original price 25¢. *Dupler Collection.* $20-$25 complete with sticker.

Appendix
Care of Collectible Paper and Products

Original magazine advertisements have become highly collectible and are readily available at most antique and/or paper shows. Many dealers specialize in old magazine advertisements and often have a good knowledge of their subject material. The original advertisements shown throughout this publication range in price between $2-$15 per ad. The rarity of the advertisement the more costly.

Many collectors of historical paper items do not realize that their collection could be in danger. It is important to become aware of the "enemies of paper" and seek professional advice in preserving any paper item. Paper documents should be stored completely flat in acid free boxes. It is not wise to place valuable paper items in plastic storage bags purchased from local grocery stores, although this practice is often seen at various shows. If moisture develops inside the bag, your valuable paper item may become worthless. Postcards should be kept in clear plastic sleeving, which can be purchased reasonably at a local paper and/or antique show in your area. This allows the card's front and back to be visible through the plastic and discourages direct handling of the card.

Never subject paper collectibles to direct sunlight, which will cause fading. Acid burn can occur from wood, wood pulp mats, backings, and cardboard. Ultraviolet light causes colors and inks to fade. Infrared light accelerates aging, causing brittleness and discoloration. Permanent mounts, including dry mounting, wet mounting, and most glues and tapes cause permanent and irreversible damage. Improper framing causes and encourages all of the above.

The greatest danger to your paper items comes from insects that like to feed on them. The older the paper, the greater the risk. Remember that paper collectibles retain their greatest value in pristine condition; anything that happens to change the condition of the item reduces its value. Protect your investment and avoid the enemies of paper.

Bibliography

Brough, James. *The Woolworths*. McGraw-Hill Book Company, © 1982.

Fortieth Anniversary Souvenir F.W. Woolworth Co., 1879-1919. The First Store, Lancaster, Pa. © F.W. Woolworth Co.

Heymann, C. David. *"Poor Little Rich Girl" The Life and Legend of Barbara Hutton*. Secaucus, N.J.: Lyle Stuart Inc., © 1982, 1984.

Home Shopping Guide "Nothing Over 10¢ F.W. Woolworth Co." © 1929 by F.W. Woolworth Co.

Kresge's Golden Anniversary Year 1899-1949. Fifty Years of Achievement.

Kresge's Katalog 5¢ and 10¢ Merchandise "The Original Parcel Post 5 and 10-cent Store." © 1913, 1975 by S.S. Kresge Company.

Lebhar, Godfrey M. *1967 Statistical Supplement Chain Stores in America - 1859-1962, Third Edition*. New York: Chain Store Age Books, a division of Chain Store Publishing Corporation.

——. *Chain Stores in America: 1899-1962, Third Edition*. New York: Chain Store Publishing Corporation, © 1952, 1959, 1963.

Snyder, Phillip V. *The Christmas Tree Book*. First published in the United States of America by The Viking Press, 1976.

"S.S. Kresge The S.S. Kresge Story By Stanley S. Kresge As told to Steve Spilos." Racine, Wisconsin: Western Publishing Company, Inc., © 1979.

The Cathedral of Commerce, Woolworth Building New York. © 1917 by Broadway Place Co., and © 1921 by Broadway Park Place Co.

The Kresge Job Ahead. © 1924 S.S. Kresge Company.

"The Story of Everybody's Store," Woolworth's First 75 Years 1879-1954. © 1954 by F.W. Woolworth Co.

"The Story of W.T. Grant and The Early Days of The Business He Founded." © 1954 by W.T. Grant Company.

WOOLCO Knitting & Crocheting Manual, © 1916 F.W. Woolworth Co.

Index

144